THE TALE OF THE TULSI PLANT AND OTHER STUDIES

The Worship of the Tulsi Plant.

THE TALE OF THE TULSI PLANT AND OTHER STUDIES

C. A. KINCAID

NEW AND REVISED EDITION

GYAN

Published by

GYAN

Gyan Publishing House
5, Ansari Road
Daryaganj, New Delhi-110002
Phone: 011-47034999, 9811692060
E-mail: books@gyanbooks.com

Distribution Network
gyanbooks.com
India, USA, Canada, UK, Australia, France

ISBN : 978-81-212-4081-9 (PB)
First Published, Bombay, 1916

2nd Impression 2020

Printed at: Gyan Press, Delhi.

The Tale of the Tulsi Plant and Other Studies
Author: C. A. Kincaid

THE TALE OF THE TULSI PLANT AND OTHER STUDIES

BY

C. A. KINCAID, C.V.O., I.C.S.

Author of:—"THE OUTLAWS OF KATHIAWAR." "DECCAN NURSERY TALES," AND "THE INDIAN HEROES."

NEW AND REVISED EDITION.

BOMBAY:

D. B. TARAPOREVALA SONS & CO.,

103, MEDOWS STREET, FORT.

1916.

TO

MY MANY INDIAN FRIENDS IN

POONA AND

THE WESTERN DECCAN

THIS VOLUME IS AFFECTIONATELY

INSCRIBED

NOTE TO SECOND EDITION.

The second edition of this book has been corrected by my friend Rao Bahadur D. B. Parasnis, who never wearies in his assistance to my labours.

C. A. K.

PREFACE.

As nearly all the ensuing sketches have already appeared in the *Times of India* and are reproduced with the kind permission of its editor, no preface is really required. Since, however, the article on Marathi proverbs gave, when published, some offence to Deccani readers, I take this opportunity of assuring them that the suggestion that Maharashtra meant the country of the Mhars (Mahar Rashtra) was not mine at all. It may be found at p. xxiii of the Preface to Molesworth's Dictionary. I am glad, however, to state that my old and valued friend Sir Ramkrishna Bhandarkar, C.I.E., has convinced me that Molesworth's derivation must on philological grounds be incorrect. I have therefore rewritten the latter half of the said article. The other articles are practically unaltered.

C. A. K.

"La muraille chinoise que l'ignorance avait élevée. . . s'abaisse de plus en plus. Quand elle aura disparu, on sera bien étonné de découvrir que derrière il y avait tant de braves gens. L'œuvre de démolition est commencée depuis longtemps. En donnant ces pages de mon journal écrites sur le sol même de l'île inconnue j'y vais de mon petit coup de marteau."

Pierre de Coulevain.

(L'île inconnue.)

CONTENTS

THE TALE OF THE TULSI PLANT.

I DARE say that it has often happened that a young Englishman riding past an Indian's house has seen a small plant growing in a pot just opposite the door and has enquired its name. The answer has been that it is the Tulsi, a plant sacred to Vishnu. If incurious, this answer has satisfied the questioner. If curious to probe into the secrets of the world around him, he will have returned home and searched for the word Tulsi in Molesworth's dictionary. Therein it is written that the Tulsi is the Basil plant or "Ocymum Sanctum." If Basil be traced in the leaves of Webster, the searcher will learn that Basil is derived from the Greek word basilikon, meaning kingly, and that the Basil plant has in France been styled *la plante royale* and in Germany the *könig's kraut.* The next stage will be a pursuit for the Greek words basilikon dendron in the pages of Liddell and Scott; but here the pursuit will be vain, for the term was unknown in classical Greece. As it is not unlikely that no further clue will be forthcoming, I have ventured to write the present article in the hope of throwing some light on the subject.

By the kindness of a friend* I have been supplied with two extracts which show that in Italy and in Greece the Basil plant was credited with certain

* Mr. S. M. Edwardes, I.C.S.

strange occult properties. In the second part of the Secrets of Alexis of Piedmont, translated by W. Ward, 1563, there is this entry:—

"To make a woman shall eate of nothing that is set upon the table. Take a little greene Basill and when men bring the dishes to the table put it underneth them, yet the woman perceive it not, for men saye that she will eate of none of that which is in the dish whereunder the Basill lieth."

In "The Cyclades" by P. Bent there occurs the following passage:—

"I have frequently realized how much prized the Basil is in Greece for its mystic properties. The herb, which they say grew on Christ's grave, is almost worshipped in the Eastern Church. On St. Basil's Day women take sprigs of this plant to be blessed in Church. On returning home they cast more on the floor of the house to secure luck for the ensuing year. They eat a little with their household, and no sickness, they maintain, will attack them for a year. Another bit they put in the cupboard and firmly believe that their embroideries and silken raiment will be free from the visitation of rats, mice and moths for the same period."

We find too a reference to the Basil in Keats' "Isabella." Therein, it will be remembered, that Isabella after exhuming the murdered Lorenzo's head:—

> "(She) wrapped it up; and for its tomb did choose
> "A garden pot, wherein she laid it by
> "And covered it with mould, and o'er it set
> "Sweet Basil, which her tears kept ever wet."

But as neither classical Greece nor Rome can help us to explain the origin of the Tulsi's or Basil's sanctity let us return to India. And here we shall not be disappointed. For this is the tale that is told in the Padma Purana by Naradmuni* to King Prithuraj. One day when Indra went to seek for Shiva in Kailas, his heaven, Indra saw no one except a man of terrifying aspect, of whom he asked whither Shiva had gone. The man stood silent, although Indra repeated several times the question. Then Indra grew angry and hurled at him his thunderbolt. The man disappeared and in his place stood Shiva, who was so wroth, that to save Indra's life, Brahaspati, the priest of the gods, had to throw himself at Shiva's feet, and thus obtain Indra's life as a boon. But the lightning, that in Shiva's wrath had, to kill Indra, flashed from his third eye, could not return whence it came, so Shiva, that Indra might not be struck, hurled it into the sea where the Ganges meets it. And of the union of that lightning with Ocean a boy was born whom Brahmadev caught up to himself and to whom he gave the name of Jalandhar or Sea-seized. And to him Brahmadev gave the boon that by no hand but Shiva's could he perish. Jalandhar grew up strong and tall and conquered the kings of the earth and in due time married Vrinda, the daughter of the demon Kalnemi. And under the rule of Jalandhar the demons, who had been by the gods driven into hell, came forth and urged Jalandhar to

* Naradmuni was the son of Brahmadev, and, as the tale shows, the mischief-maker of the gods. The word is even now used as a synonym for a mischief-maker. In this tale, as I have no Sanskrit, I am indebted to a translation kindly made for me from the Sanskrit into Marathi by Shastri Moreshwar Dikshit of Poona.

make war on them. And by Rahu*, his messenger, Jalandhar ordered Indra to hand over the jewels which had sprung from the churning of Ocean. But Indra refused saying that Ocean had sheltered the enemies of the gods and that, therefore, they had rightly churned Ocean and had robbed him of his jewels.

So Jalandhar and the demons fought Indra and the gods in the forest of Nandan, and as the gods fell Brahaspati revived them with the nectar plant that grew on the slopes of Dronadri. But Jalandhar hurled Dronadri into the sea and the terrified gods fled for shelter into the caves that pierce the sides of Suwarna or the gold mountain. Then the gods prayed to Vishnu and he came forth to rescue them, but against Jalandhar Vishnu's thunderbolts were harmless because of the boon granted by Brahmadev. And Jalandhar with his mace smote Vishnu's eagle so that it reeled, and Vishnu stayed the fight and granted Jalandhar a boon. And he asked Vishnu to bring Laxmi and live with him on earth in his place. Vishnu perforce consented and Jalandhar ruled as undisputed lord of the three worlds. The rain fell at the appointed times, poverty was unknown, the ryots lived freed alike from misery and sickness,† and all but the gods rejoiced under the sway of Jalandhar. But Naradmuni, the mischief maker, went to his court. He saluted Naradmuni and asked him whence he came. He replied that he had come from

---

* Rahu was the messenger of the demons. Originally a Mang by caste, his head was cut off by Vishnu. Rahu and Ketu, the severed part of him, now amuse themselves by swallowing the Sun and Moon and so causing Eclipses.

† The writer regards Jalandhar's rule merely as a change of dynasty.

Kailas where he had seen Shiva and Parvati and herds of Kamdhenus, or Cows that grant desires, and forests of Kalpavriksh, or trees that fulfil wishes, and masses of Chintamanis or the jewels that bestow favours, and that he had come to see whether in the three worlds there was any wealth like that of Shiva or any beauty like that of Parvati. And in this wise Naradmuni stirred up hatred against Shiva in Jalandhar and he sent by Rahu a message calling on him to hand over his wife and wealth, and covering himself with ashes to live for ever in the burning ground. Then Shiva was exceedingly wroth, and from his eyebrow there came forth a terrible shape with a man's body and a lion's face. It ran to eat up Rahu, but Shiva, as he was a herald, saved him, and ordered the shape to eat up its own arms and legs. And then to console it Shiva granted it the boon of being always at the door of his temples and gave it the name of Kirtimukh or Fameface.* But he sent Rahu with a scornful answer back to Jalandhar and he and Shiva fought each other on the slopes of Kailas.

But even Shiva could not prevail against Jalandhar so long as his wife Vrinda remained chaste. So Vishnu, who had lived with her and Jalandhar and had learnt this secret, plotted her downfall. One day when she, sad at Jalandhar's absence, had left her gardens to walk in the waste beyond, two demons met her and pursued her. She ran with the demons following until she saw a Rishi at whose feet she fell and asked for shelter. The Rishi with his magic burnt up the demons into thin ash. Vrinda then asked him for news of her husband. At once two apes

* This Kirtimukh is still carved on the door of the Shivaite Temples.

laid before her Jalandhar's head, feet and hands. Vrinda, thinking that he was dead, begged the Rishi to restore him to her. The Rishi said that he would try, and in a moment he and the corpse had disappeared and Jalandhar stood by her. She threw herself into his arms and they embraced each other. But some days later she learnt that he with whom she was living was not her husband, but Vishnu who had taken his shape. And she cursed Vishnu and foretold that in a later Avatar the two demons, who had frightened her, would rob him of his wife; and that to recover her he should have to ask the aid of the apes who had brought Jalandhar's head, feet and hands. Vrinda then threw herself into a burningpit. And Jalandhar, once Vrinda's chastity had gone, fell a prey to Shiva's thunderbolts. Then the gods came forth from their hiding place and garlanded Shiva. The demons were driven back to hell and men once again passed under the tyranny of the gods. But Vishnu came not back from Vrinda's palace, and those who sought him found him mad for grief, rolling in her ashes. Then Parvati, to break the charm of Vrinda's beauty, planted in her ashes three seeds. And they grew into three plants, the Tulsi, the Avali and the Malti, and by the growth of these seeds Vishnu was released from Vrinda's charm. Therefore, he loved them all, but chiefly the Tulsi plant, which, as he said, was Vrinda's very self. Yet was her curse fulfilled. For the Avatars of Vishnu were these: Matsya or the fish, Kurma or the tortoise, Varaha or the boar, Narasinh or the lion, Waman or the dwarf, Parashurama or the lord of the axe, and then Ramchandra the world conqueror.

In this 7th incarnation the two demons, who had frightened Vrinda, became Ravan and his brother Kumbhakarna. And they bore away Sita to Lanka. And to recover her Ramchandra had to implore the help of the two apes who had brought her Jalandhar's head and hands, and in this incarnation they became Hanuman and his warriors. But in the 8th incarnation which was that of Krishna, the Tulsi plant took the form of a woman Radha, and as such wedded on Kartik Sud twelfth, the gay and warlike lord of Dwarka. And thus it is, when the Indian nights grow crisp with the coming cold, the women, from the full-moon of Ashwina to the full-moon of Kartik light high above their houses the Akashdiwa or heavenly lamp, and so celebrate the wedding of Krishna* and Radha and the reconciliation of Vishnu with the demon-lady whom he wronged. Good luck attends the house of her who waters the Tulsi plant, and the worship of Vishnu is incomplete, unless the Tulsi plant is placed on the black Shaligram stone which, picked up in the bed of the Gandak river, is regarded as the symbol of the godhead.

Lastly, the comic element is not wholly absent, for when in Marathi one wishes to say that one must somtimes do evil that good may come, it is best expressed by the saying "tulsiche mulant kanda lavavalajato" (One must place an onion in the root of the Tulsi plant). While an unworthy son of a noble father (*patris heroi filius degener*) is styled bhang growing in a Tulsi (to tulshint bhang ahe).

---

* Krishna was married to Radha under the name of Damodar. The story goes that in order to restrain his youthful frolics, his foster mother, Yeshoda, tied him with a rope (dam or dave) round the stomach "udar" to a stone mortar.

THE TALE OF THE SHAMI TREE.

In my last chapter I gave my readers the story of the Tulsi plant. I now venture to put before them the legends that have gathered round the Shami tree or Mimosa Suma, a big thorny tree not unlike the babul. One may see it both in the Deccan and in Kathiawad and in the latter province rags are often tied to it as votive offerings. The first legend, which is that of its metamorphosis from a young girl, is given in Chapter 33 of the Kridakand from the latter half of the Ganeshpurana. One day when Naradmuni* was walking up and down the three worlds he came to Indra's capital, Amraoti. Indra rose and saluted, and in the course of their talk asked Naradmuni whether he knew and, if so, he would tell him the story of Aurava, the Rishi. And Narad told him the following tale: "Once upon a time there lived in Malva a Brahman named Aurava, who was ripe with the learning of the Vedas. His face shone like the sun and his knowledge was such that all gold to him was dross and all that his mind willed he could do, for he could create, cherish or destroy as he listed. By his wife, Sameghan, he had born to him late in life a beautiful daughter, called Shami, to whom he gave all her heart's desire. When she was seven years old he wedded her to the Rishi Dhoumya's son,

* My readers will remember that Naradmuni is the mischief-maker of the gods. It was he who tempted Jalandhar to make war on Shiva.

Mandar, who lived and studied with a preceptor, named Shaunak. After their wedding the girl and boy parted until they had reached the fulness of youth. Then Mandar went to the house of Aurava the Rishi, and taking Shami from her father's house, set forth with her to the house of Shaunak, his guru. On the road they passed by the house of a mighty Rishi or sage, called Bhrushundi. He was the untiring worshipper of Ganpati and by his austerities he had won from the god the boon that he also might grow a trunk from his forehead. When Shami and Mandar saw the trunk-faced sage they burst out laughing, and he in anger cursed them. And the curse was that they should become trees from which even animals turned away. And so Mandar became the Mandar tree, whose leaves no beast will eat, and Shami the Shami tree on whose thorns no bird may rest. Some days passed and the guru Shaunak, anxious that Shami and Mandar tarried, went in search of them. He went first to the house of the sage Aurava and heard that they had left it. Then Aurava and Shaunak searched everywhere until they came to the hermitage of Bhrushundi and learnt of the curse that had befallen Mandar and his bride. The two old men then practised such terrible austerities in Ganpati's honour that he revealed himself to them, 10 cubits high and riding on a lion. They begged of him as a boon that he should restore to them Shami and Mandar. But the god feared to displease his disciple Bhrushundi and granted them instead that the two trees should be honoured throughout the three worlds and that neither Shiva's nor his own worship should be complete without their presence.

When the god vanished Shaunak went his way, but Aurava in despair left his mortal covering and became the fire which lies hidden within the trunk of the Shami tree."

Such was the tale told by Naradmuni to Indra, but to this day when sacrifices are burnt in the temples of Shiva and Ganpati, their priests rub together pieces of the Shami tree and the hidden fire within it leaps out and kindles the sacrifice.* And no worship is complete without the Shami leaves and the Mandar flowers being present on the altar.

A second and later legend and one which is better known connects the Shami tree with the famous Pandav brothers. Students of the Mahabharata will remember how Yudhishtira, tempted by Naradmuni to perform the Rajsuya, incurred the envy of his cousin Duryodhana; how Duryodhana, to gratify his jealousy, played with Shakuni's aid at dice with Yudhisthira; how Yudhishthira lost all he possessed, kingdom, wealth, wife and brothers; how Duryodhana's father, Dhritarashtra, gave them to him all back, and, lastly, how the infatuated Pandav again gambled with Duryodhana and had to pay as forfeit twelve years, residence in the woods with his wife and brothers and then a thirteenth year of disguise in a distant country. If the disguise were penetrated the Pandavs were to stay another twelve years in exile. When the first twelve years, those of the forest life, had passed, the Pandavs with Draupadi cast about where the thirteenth year should be spent and they fixed on Viratnagar,† the

* This may be seen at any temple of Shiva.

† This name is preserved in Vairat fort close to Wai.

modern Wai, where the temples are still mirrored in the waves of the Krishna. And Yudhishthira disguised himself as a gambler and Bhima as a cook and Arjuna as a eunuch* and Nakula as a groom, and Sahadeva as a milkman and lastly Draupadi as a waiting woman. And at the Court of King Virata, they dwelt until the years of exile were over. But before assuming their disguises the Pandavs hid their weapons inside a Shami tree. Here let me give a translation of the original passage:†

Arjuna said ' O king, I see a tall Shami tree on a rising ground ; it is well if we hang our weapons on it. For, see, because of the great thorns that spread round it on every side it is hard for any one to climb it. And again there is no one here now to see what we are doing. The tree too is in a lonely spot wherein live snakes and wild beasts, and as it is used as a burning ground, there is but small fear of men wandering hither. Therefore, let us place our weapons on this tree and then let us go to Viratnagar and as already resolved let us each on his own errand complete there the days of exile.' And in this wise Arjuna spoke to Yudhishthira and all the Pandavs got ready to give up their weapons. First Arjuna loosed the bow string of the mighty Gandiva‡. Ah ! Gandiva, who

---

* Arjuna was condemned to be a eunuch because he slighted the beauty of Urwashi Indra's queen.

† I have not translated from the Sanskrit but from Messrs. Datar and Modak's admirable Marathi rendering. The book has been published at great expense by Messrs. Chiplunkar and Co's. at the Indira Press, Poona, and the second half of the rendering is delayed for want of funds. I would venture to appeal to the Marathi reading public to assist by purchasing the part already translated, in the publication of the second half.

‡ The name of Arjuna's bow given to him by Agni when he fought against Indra.

can describe it? For by the strength of it did Arjuna in his chariot subdue the gods and all men and all countries. Then Yudhishthira freed the gut of the bow by whose aid he had guarded the land of the Kurus. Next Bhima undid the fastenings of his bow. O king![*] with this bow had Bhima the mighty defeated in battle the Panchalas and the lord of Sindhu and in the hour of victory he had singlė haned humbled a multitude of warriors. For, O king! the shock of that bow was like the thunderbolt that falls upon and shatters the hill crests. Next beautiful sweet-tongued Nakula untied the bow with which he had conquered the lands of the West. And last of all Sahadeva[†] unstrung the bow by whose help he had won the kingdoms of the Deccan. In this wise the Pandavs freed their bow strings and they laid down their bows and their bright swords, their jewelled quivers and their piercing arrows.

Yudhishthira gathered them together and told Nakula to climb the tree. And Nakula did so and in the holes and crevices where the arms might best lie and where the rain would not reach them, there he placed them and tied them with strong cords. Then the Pandavs tied a corpse to the tree thinking that its sight and smell would keep men from wandering thither. Then they walked towards Viratnagar and on the road they said to the shepherds and cowherds and others whom they passed: 'According to the custom of our family we have

---

* The king here is king Janmejaya to whom in the forest the sage Vaishampayan told the deathless tale of the heroes of the house of Bharata.

† The conquests of Sahadeva survive in the name of Coromandel, Kuru—Mandal the province of the Kurus.

tied to that tree the corpse of our mother, dead at the age of 180*. So the Pandavs guarded against the evil thoughts that arise in men's minds and that they might there pass the thirteenth year of exile they entered the mighty city of Viratnagar.'

There is yet a third tale that connects the Shami tree with Raghu, the grandfather of Ramchandra. It runs that one day a young sage called Kautsa quarrelled violently with his guru or teacher Vartantu and wished to leave him. But Vartantu before he let him go dunned him for fourteen crores of rupees as the price of his apprenticeship. Kautsa went to the court of king Raghu of Ayodhya to beg his master's fee. But he came at an unhappy time. King Raghu had just held a mighty sacrifice and he had given everything he possessed to the Brahmanas who had assembled. So that when Kautsa came to king Raghu's court the generous prince was reduced to dine off earthen plates. Kautsa's heart sank within him when he saw king Raghu's poverty nevertheless he disclosed his object. The prince called his treasurer but in vain. The treasure room was as bare as Mrs. Hubbard's cupboard. In despair king Raghu prepared to raid Indra's capital Amraoti and rob him of the fourteen crores asked for by Kautsa. Just at this time Naradmuni came to Ayodhya and after the customary salutation enquired and learnt the cause of king Raghu's preparation. He at once went to Amraoti and told Indra. The latter alarmed at the resolve of the desperate Kshattriya sent for the god Kubera, his treasurer and the lord of all wealth, and

* The extraordinary age of the old mother seems to have been accepted as quite an ordinary statement.

made him for three and-a-half ghatkas the same night shower gold on Ayodhya. And the gold all fell in one place where a giant Shami tree stood. And next morning, the 10th of Ashwin Sudh, the day chosen by his astrologers as auspicious for his advance against Indra, king Raghu saw masses of gold heaped all-round the tree. He called Kautsa and told him to take it away. But the sage said that he wanted but the fourteen crores with which to pay Vartantu. And taking them he went his way. But the proud Kashattriya refused to touch what had been obtained for the needs of a Brahmana and the rest of the gold lay there that all who wanted it might help themselves. And still on the 10th Ashwin Sudh day that king Raghu should have started for Amraoti and better known as Dassara from Dasha 10th, Maratha villagers keep alive his memory. For first worshipping the trunk of the Shami tree they cut off its branches and mixing them with earth, sesamum flowers, Apta leaves, and bajri ears they offer them to Ganesha who turns them, it is fancied, into gold. The heap is then taken to the village boundary and is there looted by the men and boys of the village. And this is the ceremony of the *simolanghan.*

But there is a still stranger sequel. For in honour of his grandfather, Ramchandra chose also for his expedition against king Ravan of Lanka the 10th of Ashwin Sudh and before starting prayed to the Shami tree for success. And century after the Rajput Kings have prayed to the Shami tree and led forth against each other or the Mleccha, the heroes of Mewar and Marwar. And following them the Maratha captains did likewise and on Dassara started forth on their raids. Then in the Peshwa's time when warfare became more scientific and organised campaigns took the place of razzias, the Dassara became a great festival on which the Peshwa distributed amid regal state dresses of honour to the Indian princes. And this custom when the Peshwai passed away was continued by the English Resident until in the late Empress' time the date was changed from the Dassara to the Sovereign's birthday, a practice which continues to this day. And thus it is that when the Agent for the Sirdars and the Deccan nobles assemble at the yearly Durbar to express their loyalty to their august master, the King Emperor, they also do homage all unwittingly to the legendary sanctity of King Raghu's Shami tree.

THE STORY OF THE BEL PLANT.

The scientific name of the Bel plant is Aigle Marmelos which, as I will freely admit, throws but little light on the subject. In appearance it is an ordinary enough shrub with small green leaves and green apple-shaped fruit. In Hindu religious circles, however, the Bel tree has a very large place, and its connection with Sati, the first wife of Shiva, seems to indicate a pre-Aryan origin of its sanctity. Sati's story is told in the Shrimat Bhagwat, the tale that was told by the sage Maitrya to Vidura, the brother of Pandu, and Dritarashtra, and thus the uncle of the Pandavs and Kuravs, the heroes of the Great War.

Sati was the daughter of King Daksh by his union with Prasuti, the third daughter of self-sprung Manu. Now sixteen daughters were born of this union. And of them thirteen were given in marriage to Dharma or Religion. And their names were Budhi or Talent, Medha or Discernment, Shradha or Devotion, Maitri or Friendship, Daya or Pity, Shanti or Calmness, Tushti or Satisfaction, Titiksha or Patience, Rhi or Intelligence, Unati or Happiness, Pushti or Weal and Murti or Shape. And to each of these was born a son of various names, but to Murti were born Nar and Narayan* at whose birth the Heavens burst into music and the angels and the

* They were incarnations of Vishnu although not named among the ten principal ones.

cherubs—the Gandarvas and the Kinnars—began all to sing on the fifth note.† The fourteenth daughter was Swaha or Flame who wedded Agni or Fire. And the fifteenth daughter was Swadha whom King Daksh gave in marriage to the Pitars or deified saints. And the sixteenth was Sati and her he bestowed on the god Shiva. But of this marriage only evil came, and here I will give a translation of the opening passage of the second chapter of the fourth book of the Shrimat Bhagwat.

"O Vidura, once upon a time King Daksh planned a sacrifice and he invited to it with their pupils Vasishta and the sages and the Rishis and their retinues and all the gods and the Munis and the Agnis.‡ And shortly after they had come King Daksh entered. And by his lustre, O Vidura, the mighty hall of sacrifice lit up. And all therein seeing this king among men stood up, save only Brahmadev and Shiva. And King Daksh, after bowing to Brahmadev as the guru of all, sat on his appointed throne. But Shiva had never even moved in his seat and King Daksh felt so wroth at this that his eyes grew red as fire. And he so glared at Shiva so that those seated round expected Shiva to be consumed. Then Daksh rose and pointing to Shiva said in the presence of all:

"'O members of the assembly, what I say to you do not think that I say it lightly or thoughtlessly . . . . .'"

† The 7 notes or swars of Hindu music corresponding to the key of C Natural are Sa, Re, Ga, Ma, Pa, Da, and Ni. Thus the 5th note would be G—the note, curiously enough, on which English clergymen intone.

‡ There were 49 Agnis either descended from or including the Agni, who married Swaha.

[Here follows a page full of virulent abuse of Shiva to which Shiva replies at equal length and with equal acrimony.]

This was how the quarrel commenced and Shiva rose from his seat before the sacrifice had begun and went homewards. And King Daksh then initiated the ceremonies to which the assembled guests had been invited and which lasted 1,000 years. Sati, however, had not been present, and does not seem fully to have appreciated Shiva's explanation that external honour was only good for those absorbed in the Karma marg* and that he had really in his heart honoured King Daksh who had been too unenlightened to see it. Some ages later—for time was of little value to these Mighty ones—King Daksh gave another sacrifice. And to these again he invited the gods and the saints, the Munis and the Rishis. But Shiva and Sati received no invitation card. Sati, however, longed to see her parents and her sisters and wished to go uninvited. She asked Shiva for leave, but he refused. Thereupon she got so angry that she left him to go on foot to King Daksh's house. Shiva then relented and sent after her his retinue and his sacred Bull Nandi Keshwar. So that in full state she duly arrived at King Daksh's sacrificial hall. But a visit which had begun with a wife's disobedience to her husband was predestined not to end well. So when

* There are 4 Margs according to the Hindu belief: (*a*) The Karma marg; the ordinary path of worldly affairs, followed by the careless and the unbelieving; (*b*) the Bhakti marg, the path of devotion and austerities, followed by the elect; (*c*) the Raj marg, the path of Government, to which the elect are next promoted; and (*d*) the Dnyan marg or path of knowledge, the last stage before Moksh or release from the pain of living is obtained.

Sati reached her goal only her mother and her sisters welcomed her. King Daksh and his courtiers openly ignored her. She then in the style of epic and puranic characters abused her father for several pages and in the end resolved to destroy the vile body bestowed by him that she might no longer feel towards him any obligation. How she did it will be seen from the following translation :—

The sage Maitrya said : " O best of the Kurus (Vidura), hereupon Sati donned yellow clothes and sat down with her face to the north. She first performed the Achaman* rite and became silent and then according to the rules of Yoga, or the True Science, began the task of entering the state of Samadhi or Contemplation. She first became rigid and then united the Pran† and the Apan beneath her navel. Next by an upward motion of the navel wheel,‡ she brought them to her heart and skilfully fixed them there. Lastly, she slowly forced them through her throat into her forehead. Now, as by living with the Lord Shiva she had become well-versed in the Yoga, she was then able by its means to produce a flame that enveloped her body."

And so, the end was, the poor lady was entirely consumed and King Daksh's sacrificial party broke up in disorder.

---

* This consists of sipping water in the names of Keshav, Narayan and Madhav and throwing it down in the name of Govind.

† According to Hindu science, there are in each human being 5 Vital airs: (*a*) The Pran or air of the lungs; (*b*) Apan, the air in the lower abdomen; (*c*) Vyan, the air diffused throughout the tissues of the body; (*d*) Udan, the air in the throat; and (*e*) Saman, the air in the stomach deemed necessary for digestion.

‡ The Nabhichakra is the wheel supposed to lie under the human navel.

When the sad news reached the Lord Shiva he was inconsolable and wandered vainly up and down the earth and heavens seeking for mental rest. And at last he one day found it under a Bel tree. For, seated in its shade, he cast his eyes upwards and from the shape of the fruit which resembled Sati's rounded bosom, he fancied that her spirit had become embodied in its trunk. Now it happened thereafter that Parwati, the daughter of Himalaya, lord of the mountains, wished to wed with the Lord Shiva. And to gain her end, she had practised various austerities. For twelve years she had sat with downcast eyes inhaling smoke. Then for sixty-four years she had sat eating withered leaves. In the month of Magh (February) she had sat immersed in water; in Vaishak (May) she had sat between five fires, and in the rains she had sat without food and without a roof. Now she had all but reached her object when Naradmuni, mischief-maker among the gods, visited Himalaya, lord of the mountains, and urged him to unite Parwati to Vishnu. Himalaya agreed, but Parwati fled with a waiting maid into the desert. There she drew a linga on the sand, placed on it Bel leaves, and abandoning all food and water, gave herself up to the worship of the Lord Shiva. At last, conquered by her devotion, he appeared and granted her the boon of wifedom to himself. Thus the Bel is doubly sacred, for it granted rest to the Lord Shiva and won wedlock for Parwati. And he who worships Shiva without the leaves of the Bel will be consigned to the blackest depths of Hell for one Kalp or seven ages of Indra, each of 7,000 years. And the learned in Hindu medicine use it in many ways. The young fruit is used as an aperient. The fruit, full grown but still sour, is given as a cure for dysentery. And the fruit fully ripened is used as an astringent and an appetizer. The Bel, too, has played a part in history. For, on the strength of an oath sworn on the Bel bandar, the First Peshwa, Balaji Vishvanath, trusted himself to the tender mercies of Damaji Thorat, the jaghirdar of Patas. His trust was betrayed, for Balaji was at once seized and tortured. When reproached with his broken oath Damaji replied : "What of it ? the Bel is only a tree and bandar turmeric I eat every day." Such ignoble levity only lowered him in his fellow countrymen's eyes, and, to use an Irish expression, he never had the same name in the country afterwards. Lastly, the comparative size of the Bel fruit and the Avala (*Phyllanthus emblica*) has given rise to a humorous proverb : "Avala deun bel kadane," or as we say "to give a sprat to catch a salmon."

VISHALGAD

Gurrh! Gurh! went the big car as a somewhat unskilful hand changed the speeds and we started with a grating growling sound that put to shame the contending counsel in the Court that we had left behind. Kolhapur was our starting point. Amba was our destination. And between the two stretched forty miles of straight red road which we must traverse that evening. Away then swept the 30 horse power Beaufort that carried the Diwan and myself through the crowded city. Thc cart bullocks at Kolhapur were even less broken to motor traffic than elsewhere. Some times petrified with fear they stopped helplessly in the middle of the road just across our track. Down went convulsively the driver's feet on the clutch and brake and the disengaged engines raced and bellowed with impatient fury. At other times the bullocks at our approach seemed seized by devils and rushed violently down the steep sides of the road with a speed and ease that would have roused keen envy in the swine of Gadara.

Once out of the town we sped past Panchganga, on whose banks lie the tombs of His Highness' forebears, and after 12 miles reached the ghat that leads to Panhala fort. The great car breasted the steep winding road without changing speed and we passed under the bastions of the mighty stronghold.

Our business, however, was not with Panhala so we skirted its scarped defences and switching off rolled noiselessly down its farther side. Another hour at almost full speed along a deserted road and we entered, amid the musical salute of the Vishalgadh Chief's armed forces, that feudatory's boundaries and shortly afterwards alighted at Amba.

The Diwan and I had now reached that day's journey's end and after careful inspection of maps and histories we parted early for the night. For next morning the serious business of our trip was to begin and we would ride through the woods to Vishalgadh. At 7 a.m. next day we started and took a path that had once been trodden by a Bahmini army. Allauddin Shah Bahmini II towards the close of a successful and vigorous reign resolved to subdue the Konkan. For that purpose he sent a veteran General, Malik-ul-Tujar, who, after several raids below the ghats, thought it necessary to take Khelna fort now known as Vishalgadh. On the way he captured a fastness defended by a member of the ancient Maratha house of Shirke whom he forcibly converted to Islam. The outraged noble to gain his revenge offered to lead the Musalmans to Vishalgadh whose owner Shankar Rai he represented as his own bitter enemy. Malik-ul-Tujar fell readily into the trap. For two days Shirke led the army along a broad path, and on the third took them into the forest through which 450 years later my friend and I rode. And this is how Ferishta* has described it.

---

* Brigg's Ferishta, Volume II, page 538.

"On the third day he led them by paths so intricate, that the male tiger by apprehension might change its sex, and through passes more tortuous than the curly locks of the fair and more difficult to escape from than the mazes of love. Demons even might start at the precipices and caverns in those wilds, and ghosts might be panic-struck at the awful view of the mountains. Here the Sun never enlivened with its splendour the vallies, nor had Providence designed that it should penetrate their depths. The very grass was tough and sharp as the fange of serpents, and the air fetid as the breath of dragons. Death dwelt in the waters and poison impregnated the breeze."

As we started I quoted the first sentence of this passage to the Diwan and we both laughed at what we thought its ridiculous hyperboles. But before I had ridden 2 miles I began to think that Ferishta had not gone far beyond the mark. I have seen many kinds of country both in Europe and in India but never the fellow of this. At one time the path rose so steep before us that we seemed like Shelley's moth to be striving for the embraces of the stars. In another hour we had descended so low that we could almost hear the clang of our horses' hooves echo dismally through the domes of Eblis. And the path itself, how it twisted through the jungle here, how sheer it dropped there. Did ever lover's feet stumble over such boulders as those among which our horses strove to pick their way? When you sported in the shade, Amaryllis, did your lashes fringe such unfathomable depths? Neaera, did your lover's hand lightly play among such inextricable tangles? After two hours of blind struggling we emerged as did the Bahmani army on a small valley hemmed in on every side with hills and still known as the Badshah's Tal (the Imperial camp). Here Malik-ul-Tujar's army, exhausted utterly, flung themselves on the ground. Shirke had already disappeared and had fled to Vishalgad. Thence he at midnight returned with its garrison led by his supposed enemy Shankar Rai. They at once threw themselves on the wearied invaders and killed of them nearly seven thousand including the confiding General. Next morning the survivors dispersed in every direction. Thus the Maratha Chief made his honour clean.

My companion's interest, however, lay further ahead. So we pushed on to a place within a mile of Vishalgad fort, known as the Ghod Khind. My readers must now skip over two hundred years from the death of Malik-ul-Tujar. In October, 1659, Shivaji destroyed near Pratabgad Afzulkhan and his army. Before the Bijapur administration realized their defeat Shivaji had made himself master of Panhala and Vishalgad. Then at last the Adilshahi Government woke to their danger and sent the full strength of the monarchy to cope with it. A great force under a skilful leader, Sidi Johar, and accompanied by Fazil Muhammad Khan, Afzulkhan's son, marched against the rebel. Shivaji, overawed, threw himself into Panhala hoping to defend it long enough for his irregulars without to make Sidi Johar's position untenable. But for four months the veteran General never relaxed his vigilance. In vain the Mavalis without tried to co-operate with the garrison within. Famine began to make itself felt among the defenders of Panhala. Then Shivaji saw that he had made an error. If the Deccan was to be liberated he must escape and the plan that he adopted showed equal skill in design and execution. Lulling the besiegers by offers of surrender he late one night slipped with a chosen band from a gate still known as Shivaji's window and was well on the march to another fort before his flight was discovered. When it was Sidi Johar acted with decision and promptitude. He despatched in pursuit a light column under Fazil Muhammad Khan. Desire for vengeance lent wings to the young Musulman and as day broke he had overtaken Shivaji's rear guard. The latter's position was highly critical. The fort was still at some distance and, even if the van guard reached it, it was quite possible that the victorious enemy might enter it mingled with the fugitives. It was at this movement that Shivaji was saved by an officer called Baji Deshpande. He was a member of the Kayastha Prabhu caste, a community who claim descend from Sahasrarjun otherwise known as Kartavirya. The tale, as I have heard it, runs thus. In the Sattya Yug Sahasrarjun of the thousand arms was King of the Haihyas. In the same kingdom there lived the sage Jamadagni. To achieve perfect Sanyas he cast from himself all the passions. Among them was Anger; and before expulsion it pleaded leave to stay urging that without anger man achieved nothing Jamadagni, however, refused to listen and

Anger was cast out from him. Now one day King Sahasrarjun visited the sage's hermitage. He was absent but his wife received the monarch with fitting respect. But Sahasrarjun made her hospitality an ill-return. For he carried off despite her protests the calf of the milch-cow of the sacred oblation. In the subsequent dispute between the sage and the King, the former fared badly. Having cast forth Anger he was unable to lose his temper. But all the time smiling beatifically he received 21 wounds in the head and died. To avenge the sage's death Vishnu became incarnate in his son Parashuram and this is his 6th incarnation. For each wound in Jamadagni's head he cleared the earth once of the Kshattriyas. Now among Parashurama's victims was Sahasrarjun's son, Chandrasen, King of Ayodhya. Subsequently Parashuram came to know that Chandrasen's wife was pregnant and had fled to the hermitage of the Rishi Dalabhya. Parashuram went thither also and demanded the fugitive Queen. The sage handed her over with such readiness that in turn Parashuram agreed to do anything Dalabhya asked him. The wily Rishi then gained his object and at once asked as a boon the life of the unborn child. Parashuram was bound by his promise but he made the condition that the boy, as it afterwards proved to be, should be bred a writer and not a warrior and that for the name of Kshattriya he should take that of Kayastha as he had been saved in his mother's kaya or body. Such is the fabled origin of the Kayastha Prabhu and their qualities support the fable. For they combine to an extraordinary degree the penetrating intellect of the Brahman with the devotion and fidelity of the Kshattriya. Baji Deshpande realized his master's and his country's danger and persuaded Shivaji to press on with the main body to the fort while he with a picked band of Mavalis held a gorge against the pursuers. Shivaji with some reluctance agreed and promised that the cannon of the stronghold would announce his entry. The small band skilfully posted held the gorge for some hours and when at length Baji Deshpande fell covered with wounds the last sound he heard was the salvo proclaiming Shivaji's safe arrival.

Now which was the fort to which Shivaji fled ? The historians following Grant Duff have identified it as Rangna. Local tradition however, asserts that it was Vishalgad. And it must be admitted that the case for Vishalgad is convincing. Shivaji about to escape from Panhala would naturally choose the nearer fortress. And Vishalgad is under forty miles while Rangna is nearly seventy miles away. Again could any, even Mavali Infantry, cover more than sixty miles between midnight and dawn ? Further if Rangna gave Shivaji shelter where was the spot which Baji Deshpande defended ? I am informed that there is no defensible place near enough to Rangna for the sound of cannon to reach it. The Ghod Khind is just such a spot. On the left hand side a sheer rock falls a thousand feet into the Konkan. On the right hand side is a circle of hills to turn which would take several hours while in front the path passed through a deep cutting which might easily be held against a hundredfold odds. Moreover, local tradition finds support in two valuable documents. The first, quoted by Mr. Muzumdar the author of the Prabhu Ratnamala, is according to him of great antiquity. It mentions Vishalgad and not Rangna. The second is the Vishalgad bakhar with an extract of which I have been kindly furnished. It not only mentions Vishalgad but marks Ghod-khind as the scene of the defence And lastly Mr. Muzumdar while adhering to the view that Rangna was Shivaji's destination observes that the fight occurred near Pandharen Pani. Now the latter place is no where near Rangna but is six miles from Vishalgad. My companion and I at any rate remained quite satisfied that Ghod-khind was the scene of Baji Deshpande's heroic death. Leaving it we followed Shivaji's foot steps until we reached Vishalgad.

Of all the Deccan forts this is probably the strongest. It rises like an island one thousand feet out of the Konkan. A narrow causeway to the main land is its only approach. No wonder that Sidi Johar who followed in Fazil Muhammad Khan's wake gave up after a futile cannonade his task and withdrew with his army to Bijapur. Next year Shivaji was able to make reprisals. And it was from Vishalgad that he swooped down on Mudhol and killed Baji Ghorpade, who had betrayed his father. We did not, however, linger long on the summit. The sun was high in the heavens and the long ride back remained. After inspecting the palace which once sheltered the deliverer of Maharashtra and from which the Chiefs of Vishalgad have recently been hunted by the ghost of a restless Mahapurush, we descended the fort and prepared once again to pass through the lovelike mazes of the forest. It took us three weary hours. But even the longest journeys and the most tedious of love affairs have alike an end. Tea awaited us at Amba. Again the Beaufort car bore us along the red road. Once more the bullock carts shot like falling meteors from off its precipitous sides. And the stars had just begun to twinkle in the deepening violet of heaven as we hooted back triumphantly into Kolhapur.

---

* Kartavirya is still honoured by the Hindus. Whenever an article is mislaid it is the custom to write on a piece of paper the following Sanskrit verse :—

Kartaviryarjuno nam
Raja bahusahasravan
Tasya smaranmatren
Gatamnastamcha labhyate.

(By merely remembering the ancient name of Kartavirya of the 1,000 arms the lost thing is recovered. The paper is then placed where the article was mislaid and it reappears.

† The reference is page 72, Volume I. Readers interested in the Prabhu caste and acquainted with Marathi could not do better than purchase this book.)

A FORGOTTEN BATTLEFIELD.

As the fast mail train of the Great Indian Peninsula Railway flies along the gradually narrowing plain that divides Poona from Lonavla, it is probable that but few of its passengers observe a tiny roadside station just beyond Talegaon. The mail does not stop there and as it thunders past it is hard to read the name on the notice board. And beyond the name there is nothing else which would attract attention. A little village nestling in the centre of a rough plateau five or six miles wide is not an uncommon sight to a traveller in Western India. Yet name and spot are both worthy of more than a passing glance. For the name of the village is Wadgaon and the rough open ground shut in by the dark cliffs of the Sahyadris was the scene of one of the greatest disasters that ever befell the English arms in the annals of India.

Fully to understand the tangled politics of those times it is necessary to go back to the death of the great Bajirao, who, broken-hearted at the failure of his attempt to destroy the new power in the Deccan created by the Nizam-ul-Mulk, died on the 28th of April 1740, on the banks of the Narbadda. Of his three legitimate sons one died in early youth. But the two eldest, Balaji and Raghunathrao, both men of few scruples but great ability, played foremost parts in the history of the

Marathas. The former succeeded his father as Peshwa and nine years later, on the death of Shahu, became by the forced "sati" of his widow and by Tarabai's imprisonment of Ram Raja, Shahu's heir, the absolute master of the empire. But as he died, overwhelmed by the news of Panipat many years before the events with which this article is concerned, it is unnecessary to refer further to him. The days of Raghunathrao, however, were many and evil, and, while Balaji really founded the dynasty of the Poona Peshwas, no one laboured more effectively to destroy it than his younger brother. Indeed, during his long life, the part played by himself and his son after him, resemble in an extraordinary manner, the part enacted in France by the princes of the House of Orleans. In his earlier life the exploits of Raghunathrao recall those of the gallant prince who at Steinkirk, when only fifteen, broke at the head of the Great King's glittering guards through the advancing infantry of William of Orange. With far more claim to generalship and with a heart no less bold, Raghunathrao led 50,000 Maratha cavalry from Poona to Delhi, defeated Ahmed Shah Abdali's Afghan governor of Sirhind, and gave to the Peshwas' horse the proud spectacle of the Bhagwa Jhenda's golden pennons dancing in triumph above the walls of Lahore.

A quarrel, however, with his cousin Sadashivrao about the cost of this expedition far more than destroyed its good results. Adopting the tactics employed by Nicias towards Cleon, Raghunathrao suggested that Sadashivrao should himself lead the next expedition to Hindustan. The result was what Raghunath both hoped and expected. Sadashivrao, without military talents of any kind, was overwhelmed by the Afghans at Panipat. He and his nephew, the Crown prince Vishwas Rao, perished with 200,000 men on that bleak and bitter plain.

Nor was this all. The Peshwa Balaji was, as I have said, unable long to survive the news and in the midst of this calamitous time the vast weight of the shaken empire was thrown on the shoulders of the dead Balaji's second son, then barely seventeen, and known to history as Madhavrao Ballal. In the face of disasters due wholly to Raghunath's own jealous nature, it was yet open to him partially to redeem his conduct by displaying towards his young nephew loyalty and deference. But Raghunathrao from this time onward committed towards his brother's children a series of crimes and treasons which entirely overshadow those which a few years later brought on Philippe Egalité the execration of all Europe.

Nettled at Madhavrao's wish to take some part in the administration, Raghunathrao assembled an army and defeated his nephew's troops; and but for Madhavrao's chivalrous submission the State would have fallen a prey to the Nizam's advancing army. The union of the two relatives was soon rewarded by the great victory of Rakshasabhawan wherein Madhavrao so covered himself with glory that Raghunathrao was no longer able to dispute his supremacy. But when in 1772 the gallant and capable young prince died of consumption, Raghunathrao renewed against his brother Narainrao the plot which had been foiled by the talents and character of Madhavrao. Less than a year after Narainrao's succession he was, with the connivance of Raghunathrao and at the instigation of his infamous wife Anandibai, murdered in cold blood by the officers of the palace guard. It is satisfactory to note that this crime brought on its author nothing but misery. For shortly after Narainrao's murder his widow gave birth to a son, called Madhavrao, after his uncle, thus again interposing a direct heir between Raghunathrao and the Peshwai. Having murdered his king, Raghunathrao's next step was to betray his country. By sedulously spreading false reports he convinced the English Government of Bombay that Madhavrao was a spurious child, and by offering the cession of a large part of Gujarat he obtained their armed assistance. On the 18th May, 1775, Colonel Keating with a small mixed force of English and sepoys won, near the banks of the Mahi, the decisive victory of Arass. Some seven months previous to this action, however, the Government of Bengal had assumed the supreme control of our Indian possessions, and as the Bombay Government had carried on this war without the authority of the Bengal Council, the latter ended it as soon as possible by the treaty of Purandhar and again left Raghunathrao to his own devices. In the interpretation of this treaty difficulties occurred. Had the Peshwas and the Bombay Government approached the subject with a little good will, they would, no doubt, have disappeared. But the former were insolently elated and the latter deeply mortified at the action of Bengal. And the intrigues of a French adventurer,. St. Lubin, induced the Bombay Council, in spite of Warren Hastings' express orders, once again to attempt by armed intervention the elevation of Raghunathrao to the throne of Poona. And this closes the introduction to my story.

The expedition which was so disastrously to end at Wadgaon reached, on the 23rd December, 1778, Khandala without opposition. The force numbered nearly 4,000 men, of whom 591 were Europeans. They were within two marches of Poona, and had the army advanced with ordinary speed the capital could not have offered any serious resistance. The procedure which the officer commanding, Colonel Egerton, adopted was quite different. He divided his force into three bodies who, to use Grant Duff's words, "advanced alternately at the rate of about three-quarters of a mile daily, the march rarely exceeding two miles and the one division always occuping the ground which the other had quitted." Eleven days later saw the Colonel still at Karlee, eight miles from the top of the ghats, and neither Nana Fadnavis, the regent, nor Mahadji Shinde. the first soldier in the State, were the men to waste time. A force under the Maratha General Panse advanced with 9,000 men to harass and detain the British force until the bulk of the forces could arrive. On the 9th January, however, the invaders without much difficulty reached Talegaon about 20 miles from Poona. The retreating Marathas fired the village and a rumour, baseless as is now believed and probably arising only from the burning of Talegaon, spread that Nana Fadnavis intended similarly to destroy Chinchwad and Poona. It is difficult to understand why this rumour should have alarmed the Committee of senior officers who, from the 6th January, on Colonel Egerton's sickness, had assumed the command. A quick march to Poona would have saved it. But even had this failed no greater blow could have befallen the Maratha arms than their own arson of the capital.

Nevertheless, in spite of the protest of a civilian Mr. Holmes and of the one bright genius in the force Captain Hartley, the Committee suddenly determined to retreat secretly to Bombay. Raghunathrao who, until he heard of this resolve had been indulging in dreams of approaching kingship, hastened to the spot and in vain harangued the Committee. But the evil fortune of the pretender seemed to paralyse the brains of his allies. For all his crimes, he was probably the ablest leader of men then in India and he knew that a single resolute march would place Poona in his hands.* No arguments moved the Committee and at 11 p.m. on the 11th January, the victorious army threw their heavy guns into the lake of Talegaon and began their retreat. They soon learnt that the Maratha troops, although unable to check a hostile advance, did not lack enterprise in a pursuit. Isolated parties pushed on and seized hills in front

* Even Mr. Natu, the writer of an admirable vernacular life of Mahadji Sindia, admits that the Maratha troops of this period were worthless. 'Khogir bharte,' *i. e.* mere saddle stuffing, is his expressive phrase.

of the English force so as to enfilade it as it passed. Bodies of horse plundered the baggage and engaged the head of the retreating army, and but for the signal skill and bravery of Captain Hartley, the English force would probably have not long survived. But every charge of the Deccan horse was met and defeated by this gallant soldier's resource and valour. The whole of the 12th January he occupied, in spite of the efforts of the entire Maratha grand army now arrived to dislodge him, a low rising ground with his unsupported rear guard. And as evening fell he was able to make good his retreat to Wadgaon where the rest of his comrades had halted.

Here he found that the Committee were unwilling to continue the retreat and had already sent a Mr. Farmer to negotiate with the enemy. This as might have been expected did not discourage the Marathas. And Mahadji Shinde insisted on a complete surrender and on a cession of not only all the Company's conquests since the death of elder Madhavrao but also of the Company's possessions in Broach and Surat. In vain Hartley protested, offering himself to conduct the retreat. And, indeed, under so gallant a leader and with the spirit of the troops and the junior officers still unbroken, it is possible that the force might still have even fought its way to Poona. But the courage of the Committee had now so ebbed that Hartley's resolute words roused no echo. After a feeble demur that they had no powers to negotiate they consented to every demand made by Shinde, and they were only spared the ignominy of signing away Raghunathrao's liberty by his own astuteness. For correctly gauging the situation, he, shortly after the retreat began, deserted his allies and threw himself on Shinde's mercy. On the acceptance of the latter's terms, a treaty was drawn up and signed. The Committee were then allowed, as an act of clemency, to withdraw with their army to Bombay. I am glad to say that their conduct received there a fitting punishment. The senior officers of the expedition were one and all ignominiously dismissed, and Captain Hartley was promoted to the rank of Lieutenant-Colonel. Unfortunately, his promotion was conferred without due consideration, and on the petition of such of his seniors who had not served in the recent campaign, his pay and further promotion were suspended until they had again superseded him. Mortified beyond measure, he resigned the Company's service, but recommended by the Court of the Directors to the King, he was given command of the 73rd regiment, rose to the rank of Major-General, and was the animating spirit of the reconquest of the Konkan and of the capture of Bassein.

Such is the stirring story of the lonely station which the mail trains pass heedlessly by. Nor has its remembrance lingered with the inhabitants of the quiet village. I sought in vain with their help to locate the rising ground so stubbornly defended by Hartley, and the spot where the treaty was discussed by Farmer and by Mahadji Shinde. But battle, retreat, capitulation—all alike had been forgotten. And, indeed, when through the mists of a November evening the long purple hills look calmly down on the babul-dotted plain, on the old stronghold of the Dabhades and on the trees mirrored in the sleeping lake, it is hard to picture that they once enjoyed a spectacle unique in Western India,—the surrender of an English army.

THE BAKHAR OF THE DABHADES.

To many probably of my readers the word Bakhar will be unknown. And perhaps it will be as well to clear the ground by explaining that the word does not mean a he-goat, as I once heard it translated by an enthusiastic but ill-informed Marathi student. I am unaware of the origin of the term, but it is applied to the family histories of the great Deccan houses and these bakhars formed one of the mines from which Grant Duff took his materials. The bakhar with which this article will deal must have been written not long after the downfall of the last Bajirao and narrates in simple language the history of a family that for more than a century took a leading part in the affairs of the Maratha Empire. The book—a bound manuscript—was kindly lent me by Sirdar Dabhade of Talegaon, and as I read, at first with difficulty and then with some fluency, the old Maratha shrift, I seemed to see, through the medium of this unpretentious tale, enacted before me all the complex and striking events that together made up the history of the Empire of the Marathas.

The founder of the Dabhade family was one Yeshpatil Dabhade, Mukhadam of Talegaon, who first obtained service as the personal attendant of Shivaji. On the latter's death Yeshpatil continued to act as the tutor of the two young Princes Sambhaji and Rajaram, while his two sons Khanderao and Shivaji served as their pages. In 1689 Sambhaji and in 1690 his son Shahu were captured by Aurangzib. Thereupon the Dabhades were retained solely in the service of Rajaram, and at the council gathered to declare the latter regent, Khanderao represented the family interests. Shortly, however, after Shahu's capture, Rajaram at Panhala was in grave danger of a similar fate. He had taken refuge in that fort when it was suddenly besieged by a detachment of the Moghal army under Zulfikarkhan. But fortunately for their Prince the Dabhade family were with him. At their father's command, Khanderao and Shivaji disguised Rajaram and themselves as grass cutters and so slipped through the Moghal lines. The Prince, whose health was never robust, soon tired and would no doubt have succumbed during the flight had not the two Dabhades—if our chronicles can be believed—carried him forty miles in a single day. Shivaji, it is true, fell down and died of fatigue, but Khanderao triumphantly bore his Prince out of danger.* Needless to say the grateful Prince was not slow to reward his saviour. Indapuri, Urase, and Dhankan villages had already been granted to the Dabhades, and to these he added, at the birth of his son, the patelki and kulkarni rights of the talukas of Junnar, Harichanda, Puna and of the Parganas

* This feat has been attributed by Grant Duff, Vol. I, p. 277, to the Shirke family. And I dare say the honour of saving Rajaram is claimed by several different houses.

Since writing this the true origin of the word bakhar has been suggested to me. It is a corruption of khabar.

of Akola and Maval. And as the quaint deed ran: "If any one were to disturb the possession of the Dabhades his act, were he a Hindu, would be deemed as heinous as if he had killed both a cow and a Brahmin at Benares and were he a Musulman as if he had taken an oath on the Kaaba and broken it." And the value of this substantial gift was heightened by the title of Sena Khas Khel or commandant of the royal guards. Rajaram died in the summer of 1700 and Aurangzib seven years later. On the latter's death Shahu was released, and naturally wished to enter into possession of his father's kingdom, but Rajaram's widow, Tarabai, had for 7 years enjoyed power and was unwilling to give it up. She affected to believe that Shahu was a mere impostor and sent Khanderao Dabhade who had been his early playmate to test him. No doubt the lady thought that Dabhade would, as a prudent man, decide according to her wishes. But if so she was disappointed. For the gallant Sirdar, after meeting Shahu and carefully examining him, declared him to be the true son of Sambhaji and joined his cause. It was successful and honours rained on the loyal Khanderao. He was confirmed in the possession of Rajaram's grants although as the original deeds had been lost in the war they might well have been repudiated. And not long after the installation of Balaji Vishwanath as Peshwa, Khanderao Dabhade was raised to the rank of Senapati or Commander-in-Chief. He was now one of the great officers of State and in order to maintain his rank he was granted the Sardeshmukhi rights of the 104 villages of the pargana of Panner. The duties of his new office were first exercised in the conquest of Gujarat where he, in conjunction with the Nizam, won against the Syads the decisive victory of Balapur (A.D. 1720). He did not, however, long survive the fatigues of this campaign. On account of his old age he asked to be excused from further service and begged that his son Trimbakrao might be at once invested with his own earlier title of Sena Khas Khel. This was granted and Khanderao returned to Talegaon where he shortly afterwards died of gravel.

Balaji Vishwanath who had always remained on friendly terms with the Dhabades, had predeceased Khanderao by a few months and a struggle was shortly to ensue between their sons which was alike disastrous to the Dhabades and the kingdom. Trimbakrao had before his father's death made himself complete master of Baroda and Southern Gujarat and when he succeeded to the post of Senapati he was regarded after the king as the most considerable personage in the Deccan. As a Maratha also, he had with him the good wishes of the descendants of Sivaji's comrades and of the Deshasth Brahmins, both of whom had regarded with dislike the preponderant power of Balaji Vishwanath and the increasing number of Chitpawans in the public offices. In spite of considerable opposition, however, Shahu, mindful of Balaji's services, gave some months after his death the vacant post of Peshwa to Bajirao, his son. It was now generally felt that the contest between the Dhabades and Bajirao would not long be delayed. Nor was public expectation in error. At the first durbar held after Bajirao's elevation he proposed to king Shahu the conquest of Malwa. Shripatrao Pureshram, whose father had died about the same time as Khanderao Dabhade and Balaji Vishwanath, and who had thereby succeeded to the title of Pratinidhi (or the king's image), was a Yajurvedi Deshasth and as such a supporter of Trimbakrao. He as the Dhabade's mouthpiece resisted the proposal. He drew a just picture of the disorganisation of the finances, of the disordered state of the Konkan and Gujarat, and urged with force and truth that the time had come to consolidate the Maratha conquests. Their independence had been recognised. It was far better that while avoiding all rupture with either Delhi or Hyderabad, they should convert their present possessions into a wealthy and powerful kingdom. Bajirao, however, skilfully begged the question. Without touching on matters of administration or finance he dwelt on the great deeds of Sivaji, who with far less resources had opposed the Mogal Empire in its heyday. He excited the king's cupidity by dwelling on the indolence, the imbecility and above all the wealth of the Mogals, and stimulated his religious zeal by urging him to drive from the sacred soil of India the outcaste and the barbarian. But such a line of reasoning would probably have failed but for the transcendent personal qualities of the speaker. The commanding stature that reached the low Maratha ceiling, the rich clear voice, the bold, virile features, the dark imperious eyes that forced attention and above all the rare felicity of diction* that for centuries has been the peculiar gift of the Konkanastha Chitpawan produced an irresistible effect. And when at the close of a lofty peroration, the minister fixed on Shahu his glowing gaze and said, "Maharaja Sahib, if you but listen to my counsel, I shall plant your banner in the walls of Attock," the scene that ensued was the most dramatic in history. Regardless of the rigid etiquette of an Eastern Durbar, king Shahu, with blazing eyes, sprang from the "gadi" to his feet: "Plant my banner on Attock fort," he cried, half drawing his sword. "By God, you shall plant it on the throne of the Almighty!" †

The Dhabade, though beaten in debate by no means abandoned the struggle. He refused with curtness Bajirao's offer to share in half the Malwa conquests in return for half Gujarat, and in 1731 took the open field with 65,000‡ men. Bajirao thereupon advanced on Dabhai. He was fortunate enough to find the Dhabades' troops divided. Trimbakrao with part of the army was at Dabhaî. His two younger brothers were at a distance of forty miles. The Peshwa's intrigues were also fully successful. On a plea of watering their

---

* This strange admission of Desh sth Brahmins that their language to be perfect must be spoken by a Konkanastha finds a curious parallel in the old Florentine saying that perfect Italian was the language of Florence as spoken by a Roman—La lingua Toscana nella bocca romana.

† The phrase used by the king was the Kinnar Khand. Grant Duff has translated this as the Himalayas. The term is the equivalent of the celestial regions. And the excited Shahu's meaning, as I take it, was that his armies would conquer Earth first and Heaven afterwards.

‡ Grant Duff estimates the number at 35,000.

horses all the Dhabade cavalry deserted to the enemy. Trimbakrao, however, chained the legs of his elephant to a gun and disputed the battle with the greatest obstinacy. Indeed it is possible that Trimbakrao might have won, had not his own cousin Shingrao Toke treacherously shot him in the temple as he removed his helmet at the close of the day. This decided the struggle. And although the writer of the *Bakhar* would have us believe that Trimbakrao's two brothers came up, turned the tide of battle and drove Bajirao to Satara, where he was only saved by King Shahu's intervention, I am afraid that Grȧnt Duff's version that Bajirao was victorious must be accepted. On the other hand the victory was probably not so complete as has been alleged, and there may be truth in the account that the two brothers laid their swords before the King as if to quit his service and were only placated with the utmost difficulty.

The elder Yeshwantrao was in Trimbakrao's place made Senapati and the younger Baburao Senakhaskhel, and neither suffered at the king's hands any loss because of their rebellion. The new Senakhaskhel soon showed himself worthy of the honour. The Nawab of Surat had levied octroi from an envoy of Shahu, and the Senakhaskhel asked for and obtained leave to avenge the insult. With 368 sowars he proceeded to a camp four miles from the town and there displayed the Nawab's banner, whose followers he and his men declared themselves to be. At midnight they proceeded to the town gates, which were open because of the Kartik snan festival, and without hindrance passed through them, alleging an urgent call from the Nawab himself. Similarly they penetrated the inner fort, and capturing the unfortunate ruler, carried him outside the City, where he was compelled to surrender fourteen of his twenty-eight Mahals and the Chauth of Surat. For this feat Baburao received a gold anklet and the Dhabades a Jaghir worth annually five lakhs as well as the Mokasa rights over Umbare,† Khandesh, Baglan and the Karnatik. In the following years the Dhabades and their high-spirited mother Umabai conquered Ahmedabad, and an agreement sanctioned by Shahu and entered into with Bajirao giving to the Dhabades complete independence from the Peshwa's control restored them in a great measure to their old position. But in the course of the next ten years there occurred three events disastrous to the fortunes of the family. The gallant Baburao was poisoned in Khandesh. Pilaji Gaikwad was assassinated at Baroda, and the great Bajirao died on the 28th April, 1740, on the banks of the Narbadda.

Pilaji Gaikwad, who had risen from the post of Khanderao's trainer to that of his second-in command had been left by the Dabhades as their Viceroy in Gujarat. He administered the country with success, and faithfully and regularly paid to his masters at Talegaon the provincial revenues. But his son Damaji knowing the hostility of the Dabhades and the Peshwas, saw that he might turn it to his own profit.

† A small village 6 miles North-East of Talegaon, known as "Nawalakh Umbare."

Bajirao would not listen to his proposals, but his son Balaji had none of his father's scruples. During Shahu's lifetime, it is true, Damaji's schemes came to nothing. For the king saw through them and supported with admirable loyalty the descendants of his old playmate. But at his death Balaji, by the imprisonment of Shahu's heir Ramraja and the forced sati of Shahu's widow, became the master of the kingdom and readily fell in with a proposal to humble his only serious rival the Senapati. He demanded from him the cession of half Gujarat. The Senapati consulted Damaji, who, posing as a friend, scouted the idea and advised him strongly to fight.* They joined forces, claiming to be the champions of Raja Ram's widow Tarabai, but on the battlefield of Alandi the Gaikwad deserted his master, who was seized and confined in Poona prison. For the sake of appearances Damaji was also imprisoned, but shortly afterwards released, and he and the Peshwa divided between them Gujarat, while the unfortunate Senapati had to be satisfied with a promised monthly allowance of half a lakh, which was never paid. Yeshwantrao Dhabade, however, had had enough of rebellion, and in 1754 took part in the Peshwa's conquest of Bednore, and in the course of it died on the banks of the Krishna. His son Trimbakrao succeeded as Senapati, and was present at Panipat from which, however, he and Damaji Gaikwad both escaped.

On the death of Balaji, which occurred almost immediately after the news of that disastrous defeat, Trimbakrao allied himself with Balaji's

---

* This account should be compared with page 62.

brother Raghunathrao in his attempts to dispossess Madhavrao, his nephew. But Raghunathrao was also joined by Damaji Gaikwad, who thereupon plotted and all but effected the seizure and imprisonment of his old master's heir. The latter in disgust fled to the Nizam. But good fortune had deserted the lords of Talegaon. Madhavrao and Raghunathrao were reconciled and together defeated the Nizam at Rakshasbhawan, and Damaji Gaikwad obtained from the Peshwa the possession of the entire Dabhade estates on an undertaking to pay off Trimbakrao's creditors. This, followed by the investiture of Damaji with the title of Senakhaskhel, proved too much for poor Trimbakrao, who died of grief at Verul. His old enemy Damaji died not long afterwards, and in the disputed succession the hopes of Laxmibai, Trimbakrao Dhabade's widow, rose high. But once again the Gaikwads were successful. The widow obtained, through the Peshwas' help, a large Jaghir from Govindrao Gaikwad, but only to find that it had already been mortgaged by his brother Fatehsing Gaikwad to his creditors. The Dabhades had now ceased to have any real political importance, and the rest of the family history is more or less a continuous struggle with poverty and rapacious money lenders. The widow was helped to some extent by Nana Phadnavis, who placed her in possession of a Jaghir of Rs. 50,000. Her adopted son Yeshwantrao, however, was faced with fresh difficulties. Created Senapati by the last Bajirao, and granted a considerable estate in Khandesh, he fell into the clutches of Balaji Kunjar, the Peshwa's favourite, who secured for himself the remains of the Dabhade estate by the following ingenious expedient. The favourite directed the Senapati to raise an army, promising that the Peshwa would defray the expenses. The army was raised but the Peshwa disclaimed all responsibility, and the poor Dabhade was forced to agree to hand over his entire property to Kunjar that the latter might pay off the arrears of the clamorous troops. The Dabhade was now an utter beggar, but with considerable foresight cultivated the friendship of the English. And eventually the marriage of his son to Daulatrao Shinde's daughter gave Yeshwantrao an honoured retreat in Gwalior.

The writer of the Bakhar ends with an expression of grim satisfaction that Yeshwantrao lived to see the English Government overturn the Peshwa's rule and restore to the throne the heir of the immortal Bhosle who had first befriended the Mukadam of Talegaon. Nor were joyful feelings the only gain of Yeshwantrao. The English whose society he had courted restored him to Talegaon and to the property from which Kunjar had cheated him. And to-day within the old fort wall, which overlooks the trains and the motors that join Poona to Bombay, there lives a gallant sportsman and loyal gentleman, the first class Sirdar Khanderao Dabhade of Talegaon. By his courtesy I have been permitted to make this story public and his many friends will, I know, unite with me in the wish that one day or other his line may restore the ancient glories of a house which once ruled as all but sovereign Princes in Baroda, Ahmedabad, Khandesh and the Mawal.

THE BAKHAR OF PILAJI GAIKWAD.

I think that it may be said with fairness that there are at least three articles of belief commonly accepted, if not by all, by at any rate, the great majority of Anglo-Indians. These articles are that (1) the Indian lion is a small and maneless coward; that (2) the Gaikwad of Baroda means the cowherd of Baroda; that (3) there is such a person as a Maratha Brahmin. Nor are eminent sponsors lacking. For Macaulay in his essay on Warren Hastings has supported article No. 2. While article No. 3 derives authority from no less a writer than the great Grant Duff. Nevertheless in spite of such illustrious god-parents, the said three articles of belief must, I am afraid, be condemned as heretical. The Indian lion is a fierce hirsute beast similar in size and appearance to his Somaliland cousin. There is no such word in Marathi language as Gaikwad meaning "cowherd." And there never was and there never will be such a person as a Maratha Brahmin.*

* The Principal castes of Brahmins to be found in the Deccan are Rigvedi Deshasths, Yajurvedi Deshasths, and Kardus. Besides these there is a large number of Chitpawans or Konkanasths who have immigrated from the Konkan. A Maratha means generally a Kunbi, but it is often restricted to those Kunbi families who claim to have Rajput descent. The term, a Maratha Brahmin is therefore a contradiction in terms. Of course, Grant Duff knew this and his mistake was merely a concession to popular Anglo-Indian usage.

[Since writing this I have learnt from Mr. Karandikar of Satara, that the phrase is borrowed from Madras, where Marathi speaking Brahmins are styled Maratha Brahmins. The phrase is, however, unknown in Poona.]

Now if the word Gaikwad does not mean "cowherd" what then does it mean ? It is made up of two words : Gai " a cow " and Kavād " a small door ." Gaikwad therefore means cow door. And of the story of the name as told me by a Baroda official is this. One Nandaji, the great grandfather of Pilaji Gaikwad, was in charge of Bher for tin the Pawan Mawal. A Musalman butcher one day drove past the fort gates a quantity of cows, intending at the end of his journey to convert them into beef. Nandaji, like a virtuous Hindu, rushed out and rescued the cows which ran for shelter through a side door or Kavad in the fort wall. Now this Nandaji had a son Keroji Rao and Keroji Rao had four sons Damaji, Lingoji, Gujoji and Harji Rao. Pilaji was, however adopted by his uncle Damaji and in the end became the founder of the famous line of the Maharaja Gaikwads of Baroda.

Now, how did Pilaji Gaikwad begin his career ? I have found two different stories. The Dabhade Bakhar records that when the great Khanderao Dabhade was sent by Tarabai to ascertain and report whether Shahu was an imposter or really Shambhu's son he took with him as Naik of his *jasuds* or messengers, one Pilaji Gaikwad, and him he sent to tell Tarabai that Shahu was no imposter but the true heir to Sivaji's empire. So speedily did Pilaji go to the queen mother and return to Khanderao that the latter gave Pilaji as a reward the command of 50 horse. In the Pilaji Bakhar, of which a copy was recently furnished me by the courtesy of the Baroda Government, I find a quite different story. Pilaji was at first a groom in

Dabhade's household and was put in charge of some forty or fifty mares, which had become too thin to carry Khanderao's sowars. Pilaji, it seems, was an efficient horse trainer and he took the mares with him to the village of Narayanpur in Jawapur pargana where they shortly recovered their condition. Khanderao then gave him 200 or 300 other foundered nags which also recovered health and strength and Pilaji not only returned the horses but most of the money given to him for their keep. As a reward the Dabhade promoted him to the command of a squadron with which he was to garrison Jawapur. This pargana and the neighbouring districts were then in the hands of the Bandes and the Pawars—other officers of the Senapati. They affected to believe that the latter had made a mistake and refused to hand over to Pilaji his new possession. To compensate him, however, the Dabhade gave him two other squadrons and allowed him to establish himself at Songadh. Soon afterwards Pilaji had his revenge. In the year A.D. 1720 Nizam-ul-Mulk formed the plan of making himself independent in Malwa as he afterwards did at Hyderabad. To effect his scheme, he allied himself with the Marathas in Gujerat and decisively defeated the Imperial Army at Balapur. Conspicuous among the victors were the troops of Khanderao Dabhade, and distinguished even among those gallant men was Pilaji Gaikwad. As a reward he was emphatically declared to be the superior officer of both Bande and Pawar, and promoted to be the Dabhade's Viceroy in Gujerat. Pilaji's life for the next few years was a continual struggle. From the north of Gujarat the Imperial troops came pouring in anxious to restore the old Mogal sovereignty. From the East pressed the Nizam-ul-Mulk and Pilaji's only safety lay in dexterous diplomacy. Fortunately he was equal to the occasion. The first battle of Arass will, I think, serve as a typical instance. The Imperial side was led by Rustam Ali Khan and to him Pilaji joined himself. On the day of the battle lending a ready ear to the Nizam's emissaries Pilaji got rid of his ally in this ingenious manner. Taking advantage of a momentary success of Rustam Khans' artillery, Pilaji persuaded him to finish the battle by a grand cavalry charge. The guileless Mogal consented and away went the glittering masses of the Imperial horse. Pilaji, however, detached himself, destroyed his allies' guns and then charged with his Maratha lancers into the rear of Rustam Ali's squadrons. They were utterly defeated and Rustam Ali stabbed himself to avoid capture. Events, however, which were seriously to affect Gujarat, had been rapidly ripening in another quarter. Balaji Vishwanath Peshwa and Khanderao Dabhade died in 1720 and 1721, shortly after the victory of Balapur. Between their sons Bajirao and Trimbakrao there smouldered a rivalry, which in 1731 flared into civil war. The rival armies met near Dabhai and Trimbakrao was killed and his army routed. In its ranks was Pilaji Gaikwad. He fought like a gallant soldier, lost his eldest son Sayajirao and was himself severely wounded. He did not, however, long survive. The emperor taking advantage of the quarrels of the Marathas sent Abhai Sing* of Marwad to recover Gujarat. He recovered Baroda and then pretended to negotiate for a partition of the province. While Pilaji listened, the pretended emissary stabbed him to the heart. He was carried to Saoli in a palki and his body was burnt at Karanjal on the banks of the Nerbadda. In estimating his character, no great task confronts us. He was a gallant soldier and faithful servant, who, if he was treacherous in his master's interest's disdained to be so in his own. His eldest surviving son and successor Damaji presents a harder task. If the writer of the Dhabade Bakhar be believed there is scarcely a human vice of which he was not the possessor nor any baseness of which he was not capable. He was the fiend incarnate, the Mephistopheles—to use the essayist's phrase—of the cruel sneer and iron eye. But when we turn to the Gaikwad Bakhar, we can scarcely believe our senses so great has been the transformation. The double-dyed villain has been completely whitewashed. Satan has resumed his old place in the forefront of the Archangels. So far from Damaji being stained by any blot of treachery his was the noble character which suffered long years of imprisonment sooner then desert his master. Yet, I think, that we shall not be far wrong if we adopt the maxim of the publican in Silas Marner and judge that the truth lies somewhere between the two. Damaji seems to have been a bold, aspiring, unscrupulous man, whose keen judgment

* The Bakhar mentions Dokalsing as the author of the assassination. I think this must be a mistake and I have followed Grant Duff.

admirably suited to the times, enabled him to thrive exceedingly. Had he been a Frenchman of the early years of the 19th century, he would in all probability have risen to be a marshal of the empire or even to be Duke of Warsaw or King of Portugal. He would with Murat have deserted the struggling Titan when his throne began to totter, and would with Bernadotte have avoided the grievous error of returning to his old allegiance with the violets in the spring. Had Damaji been an Italian of the *cinque cento*, he would have shot, stabbed and poisoned himself into the overlordship of Seina or Verona and would have proved a serious rival to Pandolfo Petrucci and the Visconti of Milan. He would have obtained a place in the portrait gallery of II Principe; and the great secretary would have drawn his picture with the same rare skill and admiring awe with which he limned the features of Cesare Borgia and Castruccio Castracani.

The first enemies whom Damaji had to meet were the Bandes and the Pawars who had long resented their subordination to the Gaikwad. Damaji, however, completely defeated them. Pawar was taken and beheaded and Bande was forced to flee from Gujarat. The next ten years seem to have been spent in incessant conflict. In Samvat 1800 (A. D. 1744) Babuji Naik of Baramati surprised Songad and burnt it with all the Gaikwad's stores and treasure. And in the following year* Wala

* I have not been able to find why Babuji Naik attacked Damaji. Babuji was the patron of the poet Moro Pant and descended from a Brahmin contractor to Aurangzib. He was connected by marriage with the Peshwa and may have acted at his secret instigation.

Shah a renegade prince of Devgadh rose against the Maratha Government. Everything, however, ended in Damaji's favour. Babuji Naik was driven from the province, Wala Shah became a dependant on the bounty of the Nizam while Damaji was invested with the title of Shamsher Bahadur* by Yeshwantrao Dabhade, who had succeeded to his father Trimbakrao's honours. In 1750, however, there occurred events which altered the whole destiny of the Maratha empire. Shahu died and on his death Balaji Bajirao's son seized control of the entire administration. Tarabai, Shahu's aunt, rebelled and was joined by Damaji Gaikwad and Yeshwantrao Dabhade who defeated the Peshwa's troops on the banks of the Krishna. The Peshwa, however, treated with Damaji, entrapped him into his camp and then imprisoned both him and Dabhade, the former at Sinhgad and the latter at Lohgad. But here the authors of the two Bakhars diverge widely. The Dabhade Bakhar has alleged that Damaji voluntarily allowed himself to be imprisoned in order to escape the odium of his treachery. The Gaikwad historian would have us believe that Damaji, treacherously seized, endured his prison for many years rather than betray his master. The truth seems to be that Damaji had intended to desert to the Peshwa's side, but was treacherously seized by him that he might be made to disgorge Gujarat. The gallant resistance however of Kesharji Gaikwad, Damaji's relative and regent in Gujarat made the Peshwa decide to release his prisoner. Damaji received at Dabhade's expense the title of

* The date of Damaji's investiture of this title is very uncertain.

Senakhaskhel* and half Gujarat. The other half was appropriated by Balaji Bajirao. Damaji then returned to his province where he found that Ahmedabad had during his captivity passed into Musulman hands. In 1755, however, Damaji finally annexed it to the Baroda Government.

Some years previous to this date an Afghan soldier in the service of Nadir Shah had on the latter's assassination established himself as king of Herat and in 1747-48 began a series of invasions of India. To meet them the Peshwa's Government sent several expeditions into Northern India and Damaji Gaikwad seems to have been present with most of them until the complete overthrow in 1761 of the Marathas on the field of Panipat. When Vishwasrao, the Peshwa's eldest son, fell mortally wounded, Malharrao Holkar left the field. Damaji Gaikwad was the next to follow and some weeks later the Maratha sentry on the Baroda watch tower saw a single horseman struggling to reach the city. It was Damaji himself, the sole survivor of the Gujarat contingent. The rest had either fallen in battle or been during the retreat massacred by the peasants. When the magnitude of the Maratha disaster was fully grasped by the neighbouring powers there was heard, to use the expressive simile in Pickwick, an uproar such as that which goes up from the whole menagerie when the elephant rings the bell for the cold meat. Every ruler, who had a grievance or could imagine one, made a demand on the Peshwa's Government. To make matters worse, Balaji had shortly after

* The Dabhade Bakhar places the investiture of Damaji with the title of Senakhaskhel much later.

Panipat died broken-hearted and his brother Raghunathrao tried to usurp the throne from his nephew Madhavrao, a boy of 16. Uncle and nephew took the field. With the latter was Damaji, but his skilful desertion to Raghunathrao gave the latter the victory. In the meantime, the Nizam, who had no claim to make, had wisely wasted no time in doing so. He collected an army and advanced on Poona, proposing coolly to resume it as a former part of the Mogal empire. He, however, little knew the hero spirit that glowed within the boyish breast of the young Peshwa. He mounted an elephant and rode unattended into his uncle's camp. They were reconciled and joined hands to expel the Mogals. A forced march enabled Raghunathrao to come up with the Nizam at Rakshasabhavan* as his army was crossing the Godavari. The Marathas attacked the enemy as they were astride the river, but the Maratha cavalry had already marched 16 miles and the Mogal troops the old comrades of the Nizam-ul-mulk, fought desperately in defence of his son. The attack was repulsed, Raghunathrao's cavalry scattered everywhere, and the Nizam encouraged his troops to press on and the Peshwa's empire would be theirs. It was then that the true greatness of Madhavrao's nature came to light. Distrusted by his uncle he had been placed in charge of a small body of cavalry in the rear of the army With this band as a nucleus, he reformed as best he could such fugitives as passed near him. Just

* For an excellent account of this battle I would refer my readers to Mr. Thakore's monograph on Madhavrao Peshwa which obtained the writer the Manockji Limji gold medal in 1893.

as he prepared to charge Malharrao Holkar came up fleeing from the battle. He tried to dissuade Madhavrao and urged him to seek in Poona safety and a throne. The young prince turned on him like a wounded tiger. "Then it is true" he said, "that you left Sadashivrao to die at Panipat ?" Malharrao stung to the quick could but join his prince, and as the Mogal army advanced in the disorder of success, Madhavrao's cavalry burst on them stabbing, sabring, trampling down all resistance. Few troops then in India could have stood that furious onset and the Mogal army, that but a moment before had had victory in their grasp, were hurled headlong into the Godavari. Twenty-one guns and 15 elephants were captured on the field of battle, and Naldurg fort and territory yielding 82 lakhs of rupees were paid by the Nizam as the price of peace. Damaji had fought at Rakshasabhavan and shared in the victory, but Madhavrao had not forgotten his desertion to Raghunathrao, and when in 1768 the latter rebelled, Damaji, who had again joined him, was fined 23 lakhs, compelled to support 3,000 troops in the Peshwa's private service and pay a future tribute of nearly 7 lakhs a year. Madhavrao was now supreme lord of Western India, and it is not likely that Damaji, who died* the same year, foresaw that in 50 years the Peshwa's line would be extinct, and his own still seated firmly on the throne of Baroda.

As the bakhar ends with the death of Damaji, I do not propose to drag my readers through the endless

* He died from the result of an accident while making a chemical experiment. *Vide* Elliot's Rulers of Baroda, p. 56.

struggles and intrigues of his graceless sons. It will suffice to say that after passing in turn through the hands of Sayajirao, Fatehsing and Manaji, the succession reverted to Damaji's eldest son Govindrao. Through Govindrao's son, Sayajirao, the line was continued to Malharrao, Damaji's great grandson who was deposed in 1875. The English Government looking for an heir, whom Khanderao Gaikwad's widow might adopt, fixed on Gopalrao, then a little boy, and the direct descendant of Prataprao, the youngest son of Pilaji Gaikwad. As is usual at a Hindu adoption, the boy's name was changed, and under the title of Sayajirao, he now controls the destinies of the Baroda State. If my readers have borne with me so far, I trust, they will permit to make them one more suggestion. Should they have a few day's spare time, and are anxious to see how an Indian State can be guided by Indian rulers, let them go to Baroda. They will see what are sometimes deemed counsels of perfection brought to realisation. They will see Indian judges perfectly acquainted with English law and with three languages dispensing justice. They will see the State covering itself with a net work of light railways, houses provided by the State for its officials, vast public gardens and public bands kept up by the State for the amusement of its subjects. I do not say that faults will wholly escape the visitor's notice, but I greatly err if they do not go away deeply impressed with the talents and efficiency of the group of able men, who surround the ruler in whose veins there flows still the blood of Pilaji Damaji Gaikwad.

TO MAHULI BY MOTOR.

Duty had brought me to Satara, and three miles from the City and barely two from the Cantonment, lay the little double village of Mahuli Vasti and Mahuli Kshetra. As I was anxious thoroughly to explore the spot, I invoked the assistance of a learned Indian friend. By a happy chance he had at the time staying with him a party one of whom possessed a motor car. This was promptly commandeered and the same afternoon was fixed for our voyage of discovery. It happened that of our party 3 were acquainted with Gujarati, 4 with English, all 5 with Marathi. This, therefore, we adopted as the language of conversation and amid a flood of Deccani plentifully interspersed with English "Motorisms," the big car started gaily. Behind us frowned the fort of Azimtara. To the right was the English cemetery, on our left flashed by a Hindu temple surrounded by Dipmalas or lamp stands resembling nothing so much in shape as the monkey puzzles that grow to delight children in the Regent's Park and in the Jardin des Plantes. In front of us towered sugar loaf-shaped Jaranda on whose summit nestles in a little wood a small but picturesque temple to Maruti*. It is said that some 20 years ago there lived in it a sadhu of

---

* Maruti is another name for Hannuman the monkey god. A somewhat similar story is told of Shivaji's preceptor Shri Ramdas.

such surpassing sanctity that eventually growing a tail he became an avatar of the godhead—*tantum religio potuit.* Let us only hope that on translation to a higher sphere his tail did not drop off with the cold like Brer Rabbit's did in the iced water.

It does not take long for a motor car to devour two miles and soon we reached the empty bed of the Krishna river wherein a stranded ferry boat made it possible, though still hard, to realize that in a month or two the pebbly channel would be one mass of roaring yellow water striving to find its way to the far off Bay of Bengal. In front of us a notice forbidding strictly the exciting sport of monkey shooting made it clear to us that we were in the territory of the Pant Pratinidhi of Aundh. The Pratinidhi* whose title was created in the time of Rajaram and whose ancestor acted as the Dabhade's mouth piece in his struggle with Bajirao acquired this tiny domain in the following way. Once on the occasion of an eclipse King Shahu had gone from Satara to bathe in the Krishna river. With him was his favourite minister Shrinivasrao†, the then Pratinidhi, who was widely famed for his holiness and charities. Carried away by the fervour inspired by his religious act King Shahu sought in vain on the deserted bank of the Krishna for a pious Brahmin on whom to bestow a gift. Learning his wish Shrinivasrao dexterously profited by it. "I am," he said, "both pious and a Brahmin, make me the gift." King Shahu took the hint and

* Prilhad, the first Pratinidhi (the king's mirror) was the son of Niraji Bivaji's Nyayadhish Pradhan or Lord Chief Justice.

† Shrinivasrao was also called Shripatrao.

bestowed on him the 120 bigas on which now stand the temples of Vasti Mahuli*. In fairness, however, to Shrinivasrao it must be said that he derived no personal gain from the grant. For, in the same year, A. D., 1720 he gave it for perpetual enjoyment to one Anant Bhat bin Aman Bhat Galande, a man who, as the sanad tells us, was profoundly versed in the Vedas. A hardly less quaint tale gives the origin of Kshetra Mahuli, the little village on the Krishna's eastern bank. It dates from the old Adil-shahi dynasty and Shivaji gave to its Brahmins a small, and in their opinion, a too small allowance. They in the end, however, found a solution. When Shivaji died and Shambhu was murdered, the Brahmins of Kshetra Mahuli went to find the fugitive Rajaram at Chindi. There they blest him and told him to be of good heart, for in the end Shivaji's empire would return to the Marathas. Touched with their devotion he gave them instead of their meagre grant the whole inam rights which they still enjoy over Kshetra Mahuli.

As we stood and looked across the river I learnt that the temple to our right had been in 1874 built by Sagunabai, the widow of the last ruling king of Satara, Shahji, otherwise known as Apasaheb. She was the adoptive mother of the Sardar who, had other councils prevailed with Lord Dalhousie, would have been Maharaja Chatrapati, and who died not long ago at Satara and was like his forerunners burnt at Mahuli. Just in front of us, however, stood a far more interesting monument. It was that erected

* The terms of this sanad, as indeed many of the other facts about Mahuli were given me by my learned friend Mr. Parasnis of Satara.

by King Shahu to his favourite hound. The dog's name was Khandya, and the tale runs that by barking he attracted the king's attention to a tiger about to spring on him. Another version is that the dog itself flew at a charging panther, and so allowed his master time to escape. The king's gratitude passed into madness. He gave the dog a seat in durbar, a sanad as a jaghirdar, and kept up on its behalf a complete palki establishment. On its death, its body was solemnly cremated, and its *asti* or charred bones committed to the earth on the banks of the sacred river. Over them was erected a monument surmounted by a red stone image, which has lasted for over 150 years. The dog's image is unfortunately much defaced, but a small sculpture at the side still preserves for our eyes the artist's conception. For there a marvellous hound prances through the ages—wonderful, awe-inspiring, tiger-tearing. Surely no dog save that of Odysseus ever had a more enduring memorial. A few steps brought us into the very centre of the little village. On our left, rose the great temple of Vishveshwar erected at a cost of ten lakhs by Shrinivasrao, the village founder. At its entrance a mighty basalt bull seems to struggle through the river sands, and within its vestibule there hangs a bronze bell which, taken from a Portuguese church near Bassein, once swung to call the godly to worship and sinners to repentance, and now is tolled instead to rouse the drowsy god and scare the all too wakeful demons*. Just

* This idea is expressed in the following Sanskrit sloka :—

"Agmanarthan tu devanam gemanartham tu rakshzam kuru gante ravam nad." O Bell, make a sweet sound to call the gods and disperse the demons.

opposite is a temple built on a different model. It was built by Shrinivasrao's widow in honour of her gallant husband, and designed, as it is, in the northern style, bears witness unwittingly to the onward march of the Maratha armies. In front of us and across the Krishna rose the splendid flight of 35 steps leading to the temple of Rameshwar built by Parashuram Angal of Dehgaon. At its side and as if clinging to the main staircase may be seen another flight of steps which start firmly from the river bed, and then unfinished lose themselves in the sands of the bank above. The flight was begun and left unfinished by Bajirao Raghunathrao, the last of the Poona Peshwas, and to the curious affords a striking simile to his own career. This prince, destined to such strange vicissitudes, was born at Dhar in December A.D. 1775. When he was but 9 years old, his father, weary of war and failures, and disgusted with the treaty of Salbai,† died at Kopargaon on the banks of the Godavery. For the next eleven years Bajirao lived with his mother, but on her death in 1793 the all powerful regent Nana Phadnavis seized her sons and incarcerated them as State prisoners. In the meantime, the young Peshwa Madhavrao, Bajirao's first cousin, once removed, had reached the age of 21, but him, too, the regent detained in jealous seclusion. The two relatives began to correspond until Nana Phadnavis discovered their secret, and so bitter were his reproaches that the young Peshwa goaded to madness, threw himself from his palace terrace into the court-yard below. This unforeseen event gave the throne to Bajirao.

† A village near Gwalior.

Everything seemed to point to a prosperous reign. His early childhood had been passed among the English with whom his father had so often been allied. Nature, too, had lavished on him her gifts. Even the tall envoys of Britain were struck by his bearing and commanding stature, and in Maratha eyes, no surer archer not bolder horseman shot or rode in the plains of Gangathadi. Nor was his mind less finely formed than his body. And the Pandits were alike amazed and confounded by the erudition of their princely student. Yet just as at the christening of the Regent d'Orleans some wicked uninvited fairy came and spoilt all his gifts, so, too, the strength and learning of Bajirao availed him nothing. Vacillating and treacherous he broke every treaty that he made either with the English or with his Maratha confederates. Afraid to seize Shinde in open Durbar, he yet gloated over the screams of Vithoji Holkar as he was dragged by the Peshwa's orders through the Poona streets at the foot of an elephant. This last act brought on him the wrath of Yeshwantrao Holkar who drove him away from his kingdom, and forced him to sign by the treaty of Bassein his independence in return for English support. Detected in intrigues against his protectors he was driven on the 8th May, 1817, to make further concessions by the treaty of Poona. It was about this time that Bajirao began the building of the steps, and it was when he was most deeply involved in the schemes which eventually led to the battle of Kirkee that he had while standing on them in July of the same year, an interview with the British Agent Sir John Malcolm. The latter lavished good advice which Bajirao professed hypocritically to accept. Had the steps been animate they would have seconded Malcolm for their completion depended on the following of his counsel. But warnings and experience were alike wasted on the Peshwa. Only a few months later, the Resident was attacked and insulted. Kirkee, Koregaon and Ashta followed. The steps were never completed. And the empire of the Peshwas passed away from among the kingdoms of the earth.

We then passed on to the bed of the river wherein two Shivlingas lying side by side mark the spot where King Shahu's remains were committed to the earth. The reason why there are two instead of one is somewhat quaint. It happened that shortly after Shahu's cremation his Shivlinga was washed away. Another was built there in its stead. But when some years later the first Shivlinga was found lying buried in the sands, it was unearthed and placed by the side of its substitute. Just below the Shivlingas is a small statue of an Indian lady that marks the sati of Shahu's widow, Sakvarbai. She was a daughter of the turbulent house of Shirke, and during her husband's declining years she had hoped after his death to continue her influence by the adoption of an infant son. But she had to reckon with the malice of Tarabai, the widow of Rajaram, Shahu's uncle. She gave out that Ram Raja, son of Shivaji II, and nephew of Shahu, still survived in concealment. Furious at what she deemed to be an imposture Sakvarbai intrigued with Damaji Gaikwad to secure her position. But there was yet another player in the game, Balaji Bajirao Peshwa.

He knew of both the ladies' designs and turned them to his own profit. Although during Shahu's last illness, Balaji lingered in an agony of indecision yet when the king ceased to breathe he acted with the promptitude of Frederick. Early on the morning of Shahu's death the clatter of a thousand horse woke the sleeping Satara streets. Tarabai, Ram Raja and Sakvarbai were alike seized. By a clever stratagem Tarabai was herself made the guardian of Ram Raja and was induced to declare that Sakvarbai must become a sati. For the latter there was no escape. Previous to Shahu's death she had, in order to mask her plot, declared that she would burn with her husband. And the Peshwa called to his aid not only Tarabai but Sakvarbai's brother, Kuvarji Shirke, who, bribed by Balaji, threatened to drag her by force to the pyre. Sakvarbai, maddened by disappointment and deserted by her relatives, agreed to join her husband. She met her fate like a high born Maratha lady, and just before the end had the fortitude to give Balaji her jewelled earrings and her blessing.*

As the sun was setting we expressed a wish to see the evening ceremonies† held over Shahu's Shilingas. The pujaris looked doubtfully at me, but, assured that I was no scoffer, consented. Two or

* The ornament given by her was *Kudkvachi Jodi*, a pair of ear ornaments containing 4 pearls and 2 rubies. Her words were "sukhane rajya sambhala."

† There are 16 kinds of pujas in the Hindu religion (Shodshopachar). They are :—avahan, invoking; asan, giving to drink; snan, bathing; vastra, dressing; yadnopavit, thread investiture; gandh, anointing with sandal flour; pusph, crowning with flowers; dhup, incense; dip, lamp lighting; naivedhya, food offering; dakshina, money gift; pradakshina, going round the idol; mantrapushp, scattering of flowers.

three men carrying morchels or peacock feather fans with silver handles approached the grave and waved the insignia of royalty over the dead King's ashes. Then a horn-blower blew a wild blast to rouse his and Sakvarbai's sleeping spirits. They were now deemed to be awake and a Brahmin knelt and carefully bathed the Shivlingas and the dead queen's image. Again the morchels waved and again the echoes work to the wild horn's music. Then both Shivlingas and statuette were carefully dried. Halud or yellow turmeric lines were made on the Shivlingas and across Sakvarbai's breast. And on her forehead was placed a kanku tila or the red mark worn by the wife. For by her death she had avoided the shame of widowhood. The spirits were now fully dressed for their meal and tandûl or uncooked rice was scattered for their benefit. And once again the morchels waved and the horn blared in their honour. Then an udbati or incense stick was kindled and in a niranjan or metal dish filled with ghee a wick was lit. The incense smoke filled the whole air in spite of the ceaseless waving of the morchels and then by a strange illusion caused, no doubt, by the violet shades of the twilight, the acrid scent of the incense and the whole strange barbaric scene, the smoke assumed to my eyes a rough likeness to a Maratha warrior. A scowl, too, seemed to darken Sakvarbai's face, and I felt like the sleeper in the Gulistan who dreamt one night that he saw, blazing with anger, the eyes of Mahmud the Ghaznivide searching in vain for the fragments of his empire. One last terrific horn blast changed my thoughts. The incense smoke blew away. The pujaris rang a bell, scattered flowers and then knelt in reverence by the shrine. My friends salaamed and I, half involuntarily, lifted my hat to the memory of so much greatness and of so much glory. So intense had been the interest of the scene that it was almost with a sigh of relief that I turned back where the motor stood. Once again it whirled us past the Hindu temple and the Christian graveyard, and at my request it left me at the door of the club house. As I entered it to the sound of English voices I looked at my watch. The car had taken five minutes to come from Mahuli. In 300 seconds it had traversed 150 years.

THE FORT AT SHOLAPUR

Every cold weather the outward-bound steamers bring their loads of eager sight-seers, who on landing in Bombay, bifurcate as a rule into two divisions. The larger band rushes north to see the Taj and Agra Fort, the monument at Cawnpore and the Delhi ridge, the smaller of the two turns southward towards Bijapur and thence towards the Cauvery fall and the great temples of Madras. Off both beaten tracks, however, may be found spots which if lacking the gorgeous architectural wealth of the cities dear to tourists hardly, if at all, yield to them an historical interest. Among these spots is Sholapur. Its old fort dates back beyond human records. The town and its surrounding districts were the bone of contention over which Nizam Shahi and Adil Shahi dynasties, Peshwas and Hyderabad Nizams fought. And in May, 1818, the fort saw the last fragment of Bajirao's empire disappear, when General Munro drove from its walls the Maratha garrison.

To study the early history of Sholapur is no easy task. It must be sought for within the pages of the Ferishta and not only is the book extremely rare but the author's tale, to use his own quaint description of the Deccan valleys, is, "as dark as the mazes of love and as winding as the curly locks of the fair one." The Deccan escaped the earlier

Musulman raids that overthrew Delhi and Hindustan, and until Ramdev, king of Devgad, espoused the cause of Karan Ghelo, the last Rajput ruler of Gujarat, Sholapur, like the surrounding country, formed part of the domain of the Yadav princes. Annexed by the Afghan emperor Alauddin Khilji the Deccan supported Hasan Gango Bahmani in his revolt against Delhi. With the unity of conception which the Musulmans first introduced into Indian politics, this able tyrant formed into one vast kingdom all the imperial provinces and the petty States south of the Narbadda. But the administration of his descendants, resting wholly, as it did, upon local support, became eventually imbued with Hindu centrifugal ideas. One minister, Nizam-ul-mulk, made Ahmednagar an independent kingdom. A Turkish adventurer* whose career exceeds in romance any of the tales told by Shaharazade founded the Adil Shahi dynasty of Bijapur. A converted Canarese became monarch of Berar. Another Turk seized the throne of Bidar. And Ibrahim Kutub Shah, a Persian guardsman of the last Bahmani king, created, amid the roaring drums† and the regal state of his native country, the still remembered Saltanat of Golconda.

Sholapur and its eleven districts formed a debatable tract between the frontiers of Bijapur and

* Adil Shah was the son of Amurath II, Sultan of Turkey. He escaped almost by a miracle the massacre which destroyed all the male members of his family. He was sold in captivity and after being successively a slave, a sepoy, a general and a minister became king of Bijapur and lost, retook and finally lost again Goa to the Portuguese.

† This is said to be the first state occasion on which kettle drums were used in India. They are now indispensable.

Ahmednagar. Five and a half districts were in 1511 annexed to Bijapur by the regent Kamal Khan. And eventually a partition might have been acquiesced in by both kingdoms. Unfortunately, in 1524, when the princess Mariam of Bijapur was, in order to cement the alliance of the two kingdoms against Vijayanagar, married to the Ahmednagar king her; dowry was declared to be Sholapur and the Bijapuri half of the eleven districts.

Now the dowries of princesses have been a fruitful source of political trouble. Readers of Dumas will remember the difficulties that beset Henry IV when attempting to recover the dowry of Margaret of Valois and just as *le roi vert et galant* was obliged to storm Cahors, so the king of Ahmednagar was faced with the alternative of a penniless queen or a war with Bijapur. He chose the latter; but so far from gaining Sholapur, he lost two battles and was obliged, in the peace of 1542, to renounce all claims to it. But he was persevering by nature and in 1551 through an alliance with the Hindus of Vijayanagar—an alliance which shocked the faithful as much as Francis I's treaty with the Ottoman Turks shocked Christendom—he retook Sholapur and shortly afterwards died happy. The quarrel was, however, by no means over. Bijapur had now its grievance; for that administration repudiated the terms of the Princess Mariam's dowry and its young Prince Ali Adil Shah sought in turn Vijayanagar's aid to recover the lost province. The Hindu ruler Ramraj received the overtures favourably but unwittingly gave to the young Musulman, then his guest, great offence.* And so it fell out that instead of making an alliance with the Hindu State, Ali Adil Shah organised against it a great Mussalman league and destroyed it. But what caused the fall of Vijayanagar decided finally the ownership of Sholapur. For to cement the holy alliance against the infidel Ali Adil Shah married a Nizam Shahi Princess and with her came back to Bijapur, Sholapur and its five and a half districts. But she has a greater claim on history than the settlement of the Sholapur quarrel. For she was the renowned Chand Bibi of Ahmednagar. In after years she made herself regent of her ancestral State, and uniting the rival Deccan houses, strove, and for a time successfully, to stem the torrent of Mogal invasion. To the end unconquered, she died murdered by her own troops. During her lifetime she won from the chivalrous enemy the title of Chand Sultana. And 350 years after her death Meadows Taylor, himself stationed at Sholapur, wrote the tale of her life and called it the Story of a Noble Queen.

After the fall of Bijapur, Sholapur went to the Mogal conquerors. Prince Azam gave it to Shahu, who divided its revenues with the first and great Nizam. By the battle of Kharda, Nana Phadnavis

* The offence given was that Ramraj when taking leave of his noble guest did not ride so far with him as Musulman etiquette—more exacting than Hindu etiquette—more exacting than Hindu etiquette—demanded. From this incident and its ensuing consequence Briggs, the translator of Forishta, sagely moralises on the importance of studying the customs of the people who live round us. Ramraj's head was cut off by his conquerors, was embalmed and was till recently to be seen at Bijapur. It used to be carried round on a pole on high days and holidays and possibly still is.

won it all and wide lands besides for his young master, the 2nd Madhavrao. And in 1818, it was to Sholapur that Bajirao II's army, defeated at Ashta, retreated. On the 10th May 1818, his spiritless force was dispersed never to re-assemble, and on the 14th, the fort with its garrison, surrendered to General Munro. And so with this final flicker, Sholapur passed out of history.

The fort* has nothing in common with the usual Maratha fastness perched upon a cliff and owing less to human than to Nature's hands. The Sholapur fort stands on the open plain, and consists of a square enclosed by heavy walls and a wide encircling moat. Inside the walls are banquettes for the sharpshooters, and here and there embrasures mark where in old days the gunners laid their cannon. Jutting out from the walls are several great towers. And of two, ghastly stories are told. Under one called the Jaccha tower, a pregnant woman was buried alive. When first erected its foundations repeatedly gave way. The Brahmins were consulted, and they said that Mahakali or the spirit of time and place was angry. Now Mahakali is honoured both East and West. She is the spirit who snatches away from bridegrooms their brides. It is to frighten her that rice is thrown at Christian weddings, and it is to hit her in case she should be peeping in at

---

* Forts are said in the Mahabharata to be of six kinds. 1. Desert forts. 2. Hill forts. 3. Ground forts. 4. Mud forts. 5. Men forts. 6. Jungle forts. Sholapur, I take it, would be a ground fort. A man fort is an unfortified town like Sparta, whose safety rested on the courage of her hoplites. The same idea occurs in Campbell's lines :—

" Britannia needs no bulwarks,
No towers along the steep."

the carriage window that a slipper is hurled after the vehicle that bears away the married pair. It is in her honour that in England house-warming parties are given, that in France they hang the crémaillère, and that in India they perform the ceremony called Vastushanti. Mahakali was angry, said the Brahmans. How was she to be appeased? By the sacrifice of a living pregnant woman, was the reply. The poor widow of a Lingayat Bania was offered by her brother-in-law as the victim. She was buried alive and the tower stands firm to this day. But though the tower moves not the widow's ghost gets at times restless. And to quiet her, the descendants of her brother-in-law, now and ever since Patils of Sholapur, offer on the Varshapratipada, or first day of the new year, oil and cocoanuts, a *lugada*, (dress) and a *choli* (bodice) for the woman, and a little *dhotar* and turban for the tiny child that never saw the day. Of the northern tower, a similar story is told. There, too, the foundations had to be sealed with human blood, and a *munja* or unmarried, though threadgirt, boy of the Deshmukh family was buried alive beneath them. The blood money for the boy was a yearly grant of Rs. 15 which more than five centuries afterwards is still paid by the English Government. At the door of the Mahakali gate is a rough stone said to be the image of the goddess Mahakali herself. In days gone by she stood upright and sought all in vain to keep the English from the fort. But when on the 14th May 1818, Munro's troops marched in to martial music and with flying banners, she bowed her head in shame, and, as all may see, it droops to this day. To the south of the old fort is a great lake from which at any moment the moat can be filled with water. In the centre of the lake is a little island joined to the main land by a stone causeway and bearing in its centre a famous temple of Siddheshwar or Shiva self-created. After rambling through the fort and hearing its gruesome stories it is a welcome relief to walk along the causeway to the dark cool colonnades beyond. When I last visited it, the lake's surface was gay with lilies, and the wild duck swirled and stooped above its waters. On coming to the temple courtyard, I, as is my wont, gave a slight money offering to the priest for worship. I turned to go, but he begged me and my friends to wait a moment. We did so, and as we lingered I saw to the west sharply outlined against the sky where the sun had set, the great Warad mill. With the rear of its thousand wheels and the glare of its furnaces, it seemed to stand for some vision of a new India built up by native energy and capital and guided by western thought; while the old fort to the north rapidly fading away with the short-lived twilight seemed to stand for ancient and picturesque India, which before our eyes is vanishing for ever. Just then, however, the priest returned and presented each of us with divided cocoanuts containing in each half a few jasmine flowers. This was the *prasâd* or return present of the God, and from it we knew that my humble offering had found favour. And so, we walked back along the colonnades and the causeway with heads erect, *fausti atque felices*, for on us was the blessing of Siddheshwar.

PARVATI OF THE PESHWAS.

Near Poona, and itself a spur of the Sinhgad range, stands a hill called Parvati. It is crowned with temples and receives its due share of worship. But for historical interest it has probably no rival. Among its buildings one prince died of a broken heart, another watched his empire tumble to pieces like a house of cards. An English poet* has sung of its beauties and on its steps an heir to the throne of England nearly met his death. As Parvati is within easy reach of Poona residents and visitors, I have ventured to string together for their benefit a slight account of the famous hill. For to visit it without some knowledge is both unprofitable and uninteresting.

Like most other celebrated Indian celestial dwellings the present gods were not the earliest to live in Parvati. Before they came the old hill goddess was already there. The common tale goes that one day Gopikabai, the wife of the 3rd Peshwa, Balaji Bajirao, suffered from a sore heel and was told that the Devi on Parvati hill was swift to answer prayers. Gopikabai promised, if she got well, to build a temple to Shiva on Parvati's summit. She did so, and Balaji Bajirao fulfilled her

---

* Sir Edwin Arnold, by a strange inaccuracy, describes a conversation at Parvati between himself, a priest and a dancing girl. There are, however, no dancing girls at Parvati and never were any.

promise. The tale told in the Peshwas' Bakhar is different. For there the founding of Parvati is ascribed to Balaji Bajirao's wish to honour king Shahu to whose memory the Shivaite temple was erected. It is probable, however, that this latter story really describes the origin of Vishnu's temple and the former that of Shiva's. In either event the pious founder of Parvati was the 3rd Peshwa and it is related in the Peshwa Bakhar that he sent the Holkar and Shinde Jaghirdars to extort for her temples the sacred stones of the Gandaki river from the Maharaja of Nepal*.

The hill is usually approached by the Shankarshet Road, which winds past the tombs of unknown French officers once in the Maratha service, past the Deccan Club and a shrine to Bhairoba, himself like Parvati's Devi, one of the earlier deities. Then, it curves round Parvati lake—now an open ugly hollow—but once a beautiful sheet of water which the sanitary engineers, alas ! condemned. The lake, like the Parvati temples, was built by Balaji Bajirao, and the tale runs that enraged with the slow building of the dam he himself descended from his elephant and began carrying stones to the masons. At once courtiers and soldiers sprang from their

---

* The following idols were placed in the Parvati Temple in the year 1749 :—

1 Shri Deweshwar.

1 Mahadev (Silver) with two Golden images : one of Ganpati on its right lap and the other of Parvati on its left lap.

1 Ganpati (Stone).

1 Parvati Bhawani.

The religious ceremonies commenced on the 7th and concluded on the 11th April 1749 the expenditure on this account was Rs. 9,020.

horses and did likewise and the dam soon neared completion. At a later date Mahadji Shinde wishing to oust Nana Phadnavis from the control of the second Madhavrao took the latter to the little Ganpati temple on the Sarasbag island in the centre of the lake. While rowing across, Shinde so poisoned the young prince's mind against the old statesman that they in the end quarrelled, with terrible results to both. Madhavrao II perished in the Shanwar Wada. Nana Phadnavis died broken hearted and disgraced. But the house of Shinde grew till it overshadowed the whole Maratha Empire.

On reaching the pathway that branches off to Parvati, do not continue until the steps are reached but turn to the right and passing under a limb tree walk with me towards the North. The leaves of this limb tree are in great request on the 1st of Chaitra —the Deccan New Years' day. The ordinary Brahmin eats but one or two because of their bitter taste. But the Brahmacharis or youthful religious celibates, so an Indian Informant told me, eat them in handfuls and their bodies so far from suffering ill-effects wax stout and strong and their faces "become lustrous." A hundred yards or so beyond the limb tree is a little shed. Underneath it are kunku and shendur covered stones arranged so as to mark a grave. Its occupant was once a Mang who attended the Peshwa's rhinoceros and one day ended his career with its horn through his body. He was buried here and his disembodied spirit haunts the place. The Mhar attendant when I visited it said to me 'phar navasala pavato' (he readily hearkens to prayers) and recently plucked feathers lying close by, showed that but a few minutes before a worshipper had offered a fowl to the Mang's ghost. A sad tale was also told me of this Mang's doings. On dark nights he spirits away fair women of high caste while sleeping by their husband's sides and in the early morning leaves them soiled and helpless on the roadway. Possibly erring ladies of high degree, surprised by daylight, may have found in the Mang's ill-repute a welcome shelter. But let us leave the Mang and still go northward. Twenty or thirty paces on we shall come to the realm of Vetal* and Mhasoba. Here indeed we enter on primitive theology. In the centre are two whitewashed stones. They are Vetal and his younger brother Mhasoba who reign over the multitude of ghosts and demons that harass mankind. Round them are a circle of smaller white-tipped stones. They are king Vetal's sowars, and a larger stone to the south of the royal pair but inside the circle of the horsemen, is their Jemadar known as Bhangya Bava or as we might say Brandy Billy. Twice a month, on the full moon and on the no-moon, does king Vetal at midnight ride abroad in state surrounded by ghostly riders and ghostly elephants. Should the wayfarer meet him let him boldly stride up to the demon-king and ask a favour for at such a time he will not refuse a boon. His greatest day, however, is Mahashivratra.

* The attendant told me that this Vetal formerly lived at Gopgaum in Saswad Taluka, but that his grandfather had by bhakti or worship induced the god to come to his present abode. One night the god told him walk to Parvati without looking backward and next morning to make a mound of stones where he saw flowers lying. He walked to Parvati and behind him he heard all the way the footsteps of Vetal and next morning flowers lay where is now the demon ring.

On other occasions he but rides round Poona City. But on that night as the Mhar attendant told me "ratrabhar dhingana karito" (or as we might say, he plays Old Harry all night long). Sorcerers and especially wrestlers are his votaries and often before a wrestling competition one may, if one cares to visit the spot at midnight, see some stout youth bathe in the adjoining canal and then pray at the shrine for victory in the morrow's tournament. But whoever makes offering to the god must at the same time present a pipe of hemp to Bhangia Bawa, for he has the ear of and will "samjao the Sahib."

Now let us return to the east face of the hill glancing as we pass at the masonry post to which during the Peshwas' days tigers used to be tied while they fought with elephants. Their spirits have, it is believed, entered the stake, which is now worshipped under the title of Vaghoba or My Lord the Tiger. On the east face we shall find a stone staircase. At its foot are two little monuments, one to Nagoba—the serpent who was the wisest among the beasts of the field—and the other to a saint who lived and died on Parvati's summit. Next let us mount the steps passing on the left a Musulman Pir's tomb whose restless spirit produced litigation that greatly vexed the District Judge until finally laid by an adverse decision of the High Court. Half way up we pass two little stones each adorned with a pair of feet. The larger pair belonged to one Madhavrao, a Sadhu of the hill, and the smaller to his wife Parvati, who in 1829 committed sati on this spot.

On nearly reaching the top the Brahmins will point out to us where the Bhor Chief's elephant slipped and nearly fell with Prince Edward of Wales. At last the summit reached, we turn into the court-yard of the principal temple, that of Shiva. Opposite it is the nagarkhana or drumhouse whence wild music thrice a day issues either to rouse the god or warn him that it is time to rest. A stone bull lies as usually facing the temple hall and in front of him may usually be seen some grains of rice and a bel-tree's leaf given him in honour of Shiva. The animal has two panoplies, one of silver for the Mahashivratra and such great days and one—its second best—of copper for less important fêtes. Inside the temple the royal cobra rears its hood over Shiva's "pindi" and behind it are images of his queen Parvati and their son Ganesh. At each corner of the court-yard is a little shrine sacred to Vishnu, to the hill Devi, to Ganesh and to Surya or the Sun. And the latter's chariot drawn by a strange seven-headed animal reminds one forcibly of the splendid horses which prance and bear Helios so gaily in Flaxman's drawing. To the north is a railed window whence the last Peshwa watched the battle of Kirkee. And it is certain that nowhere else can so good a view be obtained of the straight road along which Bapu Gokhale and the Bhagwa Jhenda passed to do battle with the troops of the English cantonment. In the same court-yard is a trap-door which covers the entrance to a secret passage by which, it is said the same Peshwa, a few hours later, fled to the old palace in the Shanwar Peth.

Let us now leave Shiva's court-yard and skirting the southern wall look down the hill's edge. We shall see a vast compound girt by a ruined stone wall. This is the old ' Ramana ' or enclosure where Balaji Bajirao paid dakshina to Brahmins by thousands. The cost one year rose to sixteen lakhs and the Peshwa was forced at last to examine Brahmin applicants as to their holiness and learning. And the chronicle of the Peshwas relates in all seriousness that the Konkanastha Brahmins passed most frequently the examiner's tests.* Due west of Shiva's temple we shall enter a small enclosure over which several bel-trees hang their rounded fruit. Therein a small temple to Kartikswami covers two idols. One in marble was injured by the lightning that destroyed Bajirao II's palace and according to Hindu practice has been put on one side for a less costly but intact one. Who was Kartikswami ? He was Ganpati's elder brother but not born of Parvati. The tale runs that once Agni stole Shiva's vital essence hoping thereby to rival in might the dark-throated lord of Kailas. But the latter's fiery blood burnt the weaker veins of Agni and he was glad to cast it from him into the bodies of his own six unmarried daughters. They became pregnant and to hide their shame brought on each of them a premature birth. The unformed children thrown together in a corner coalesced and became the lord Kartikswami;* and

---

* *Vide* Peshwas' Bakhar, pages 54-55. The Peshwas were, of course, themselves Konkanasthas.

* For this reason Kartikswami is also called Shadanan. His vahan is the peacock.

his idols to-day have six mouths to show his sextuple origin. Somewhere closed by the third Peshwa, Balaji Bajirao, the founder of the temples, killed by the news of Panipat, breathed his last. But either through ignorance or wilfulness the priests refuse to point out the spot.

One temple remains, that of Vishnu. Opposite the hall entrance is a figure of his vahan or steed, the eagle. For Vishnu's incarnations have been martial princes and all the earth over the eagle has been the emblem of the world-conqueror from Vishnu's Garuda to the *aigles napoléoniennes*. On the door is an image of Ganpati and below it is the hideous face of Kirtimukh. Neither—I speak of course as a layman and subject to correction—seems really in place. As for Ganpati—*passe encore*!—for in the Deccan he is to be found everywhere from the temples of the other gods to the Shri Ganeshayanamah with which the Puranas begin. But Kirtimukh sprang from the frown of Shiva's eyebrow when he received Jalandhar's challenge and was called on either to give up Parvati and his treasure or meet the Demons in battle. And the boon that Kirtimukh received was to find a place always in Shiva's temples. However one must not be hypercritical and the Hindu architect, like the enraged naval officer in the story likes to feel that he has omitted nothing. Let us next look inside and there we shall see Vishnu himself and at his feet sits his last great incarnation Balkrishna. The latter, as the name shows, is not here in the same guise as when he fought on the side of the Pandava brothers and made Dwarka his capital, but as he appeared in his wondrous childhood and won the hearts and the loves of the 16,000 Gopikas.

To the south stands, hidding the view of the Sinhgad mountains, the outer shell of Bajirao II's palace. It has, however, no history, for it was never finished and lightning struck it two years before the English cannon blew away the Peshwa's Empire.

And now before we descend let us mount for a moment the northern wall. Poona City and Poona Camp unroll for us their vast panorama. At either end sleep scions of the great rival houses of Shinde and Holkar.* In the centre rise the square towers of the Shanwar Wada where so many Peshwas fought and intrigued, loved and ruled. To the north flash the waters of the Mula Mutha, now deepened by the great Band but once low enough to let Elphinstone and his escort escape from Vinchurkar's horse. To the east are the bold outlines of four—spurred Chaturshringi in whose side is a cave where the Pandavs rested on their way to Viratnagar. And at its feet is the spot where by a strange fatality the Peshwa's vakil met Sir Charles Malet, the first British envoy, and on which now swing the gates of the Ganeshkhind palace. Far to the south rise Torna, dear to Shivaji, and Singhad, where Tanaji Malusre met an heroic death. And between them the waters of Khadakwasla catch the last rays of the sinking sun and throw up a blaze of light amid the gathering darkness.

---

* Mahadji Shinde's tomb is at Wanavdi and Vithaji Holkar's south of Holkar's bridge.

Let us now descend, and as behind us the evening drums begin to roll scaring away the demons and warning the gods that it is time to rest, let us consider how we may escape unmulcted to our carriages. But of this there is but little hope. For, as in the poem of Propertius, beauty could not save Nereus nor his strength Achilles*, so all our wit and cunning will avail us but little against the multitudinous demands of the mendicant devotees.

* Nerea non facies non vis exemit Achillem.

A PORTUGUESE LADY AT THE MOGAL COURT.

Absorbed in the contemplation of our own splendid empire, we are sometimes apt to forget that other European nations have also played glorious parts in India. On a recent homeward voyage, I was reminded of this by the presence on boardship of a Portuguese official of high rank, tall, courteous and wholly charming. Finding that I was interested in things historical, he promised to obtain for me a recent book* published in Goa, giving an account of the relations between the Goanese Government and the Great Mogals. The promise was kept and the book duly arrived. But it was in Portuguese of which I knew not a single word. However, I had in my youth learnt Latin, French and Italian and so like the Austrian ambassadors, sent to win over Louis XV against Frederic the Great, I did not despair. Nor were my expectations ill-founded for, with a grammar and dictionary and the long hours of the outward sea-voyage, I was able to gather most of the book's excellent contents. And I now venture therefrom to sketch for readers the

* Uma dona Portugueza na corte do grande-Mogol by Ismael Gracias. I must express my acknowledgments to the learned author who, at my friend's request, sent me a copy of his work. Of its literary merits it would be absurd presumption on my part to offer an opinion. But there can be no question as to the author's vast erudition. Eastern and Western languages seem to come equally easily to him.

career of a lady who played a great part in the history of the Portuguese Indies.

The early years of the 16th century brought unexampled prosperity to Portugal. Five centuries of uninterrupted conflicts with the Moors had made all its small population soldiers. The royal house, founded by a bastard prince of Burgundy, had been unusually rich in able men. And ruled and rulers alike had with wonderful quickness grasped the possibilities of their long coast line, and had laid aside ambitions of Mediterranean for those of world empire. In 1494, a Papal Bull had divided the undiscovered earth between the Portuguese and the Spaniards, and in all directions the Lisbon Government furnished expeditions to make good the title conferred by the Vatican. Everywhere the Portuguese soldiers proved invincible, and everywhere administrators trained in the Lisbon offices introduced settled government in the train of conquest. One daring band under João de Nova seized Ascension. Another under Pedro Cabral annexed the vast empire of Brazil. A third under Amerigo Vespucci, first of the Caucasian stock, heard the roar of the Purana as it rushes towards the Plate river and the South Atlantic. A fourth under Vasco de Gama realised the visions of Henry the Navigator, and, doubling the Cape of Good Hope, headed straight for the Indian Ocean.

Probably never in its history had India, as at this time, been so helpless to resist foreign aggression. Hindustan was still bleeding from the senseless slaughter of Tamerlane's invasion. In the south, the great Bahamani kingdom, which in Mahamud

Taglak's reign, had fallen away from Delhi, was split up into five fragments. Of these, the two in possession of the South Western seaboard, Bijapur and Ahmednagar, were not only at deadly enmity with each other but engaged in constant strife with the Hindu power of Vijayanagar. It was an easy task for the talented Portuguese captains to take advantage of their distracted state, and to obtain by cession or conquest large territories on the Western Coast. While the real superiority of the Portuguese sailors enabled them to secure at the expense of the Mopla merchants a monopoly of the western trade.

If we pass over 50 or 60 years, however, we find the positions of the two countrils reversed. The immense efforts of the opening century had been too much for the slight resources of Portugal. A minority at home, unsuccessful campaigns in Morocco, priestly influence, and the introduction of negro labour had added to her distress. In India, on the other hand, the descendants of Tamerlane were doing their best to remedy the effects of his crimes. In 1526, Babar had won Panipat and, for himself and his successors, the throne of Delhi. Thereon was now seated a ruler of extraordinary military and civil talents, who after gathering into his own hands the threads of a vast empire, was in every direction extending its frontiers with the skill and the restless energy of Bonaparte. In ten years he had subdued all Rajputana except the Sesodia fastnesses in the Arawalis. A bloodless campaign had in 1572 ended the Gujarat kingdom. And, in 1581, a detachment of the Mogal army attacked the Portuguese territories of Bassein and Damaun. They were repelled by the Governor Martini Alffonso de Mello, but the repulse would, as in other cases, have been followed by an attack in force which surely would have succeeded had the Emperor not been stopped by something in his eyes more terrible than the Portuguese cannon, and more 'persuasive than the lips of their ambassadors—the frowns and the tears of a Lusitanian lady. Instead of war he made a treaty and sent envoys of congratulation to the new Portuguese King Philip II of Castle.

Who was the lady who did such signal service to her country? She has hitherto been styled Maria Makany, Akbar's Christian wife, whose tomb is still visible at Agra. But Mr. Gracias has with great acuteness and research been able to trace her origin. In the reign of King John III there was founded at Lisbon a home for orphan girls of good family. When these girls reached women's state they were shipped off to the various Portuguese colonies to make wives for the official and settlers. The ladies did not, however, always reach their destination but, like the Moorish king's bride in Boccaccio, sometimes fell into wrong hands. One of them was rescued from a wreck to become queen of the Maldives. Another, Maria Mascarenhas, captured with her sister by the Dutch, was brought to Surat and thence sold at the Mogal Court, where she became one of Akbar's queens and is known to history under the Musalman corruption of her name Maria Makany.

Her sister's fate was if possible more romantic still. In 1560, Prince Jean Philippe Bourbon, a cadet of the house of Navarre, fled from France as a result of a fatal duel, and making his way from Madras to Delhi, applied to enter Akbar's service. He was received with great distinction, given the title of Nawab, appointed governor of the royal harem, and wedded to Juliana Mascarenhas, Maria's sister. The two Portuguese ladies thus formed a strange link between the great house of Chagatai, and the no less splendid line that for two centuries overawed Europe from the throne of Clovis.*

Having saved her countrys' possessions, Maria Mascarenhas next tried to save her husband's soul. Her own palace had long been adorned with frescoes of the Annunciation, and, as a result of the new treaty with Goa, Akbar was induced to invite to his court a band of missionaries qualified to expound the Christian doctrine. Among them went the Jesuit Rodolfo Acquaviva, whose dialectic talents, according to the Oriente Conquistado, proved too much for Akbar's Mullahs. It must, however, be confessed that, if the latter were correctly reported, so to triumph was not a difficult task. They attacked the Christian religion by alleging that the Bible had originally been verbally the same as the Koran, but had been altered to its present form in order to introduce the idolatrous worship of the Trinity. And they asserted that Mahomed's

* The descendants of Prince Jean Philippe Bourbon are still to be found in India. One branch until recently held a *jaghir* in the Bhopal State, and a member of their family some 20 or 30 years held the post of Prime Minister to its Nawab. For an account of this family, *vide* Colonel Kincaid's "History of the Bourbons in India" and Rousselet makes a mention of them in his "Rajahs des Indes."

mission had been to restore the pure faith which Christ had taught. Such an allegation, unsustained by any evidence, was easily ridiculed out of Court. But the learned Jesuit's reply does not, to my mind, give proof of much ability. His criticism was purely destructive, and he made no attempt to show how the teaching of Christ was superior to that of Mahomed. Nevertheless, what the contending saints lacked in brain-power they made up for in lung-power. And as they warmed to their work, the Emperor, at whose invitation they had assembled in the Ibadat Khana, found that to conquer Hindustan was an easier task than to calm this controversial cyclone. He was finally obliged himself to flee deafened from the room, leaving the disorderly conference to continue all night until exhaustion silenced it towards morning.

Subsequent to this the Mullahs, wearied with argument, made to the missionaries what, as it must fairly be admitted, was a sporting offer. They expressed themselves willing to enter a fiery furnace if the missionaries did likewise. The former were to be armed with a Koran, the latter with a Bible, and the fire was to judge between them. The missionaries replied that they had already won a judgment in the tribunal of reason that miracles were only intended to supplement evidence, and that where reasons were as in the case of Christian truth, so clear and manifest, it was merely tempting God to ask for miracles without necessity. Such arguments could scarcely have convinced Akbar, and the distinct favour with which he regarded Christianity must only have been due to his wife's pressure. On one occasion he did homage to the crucifix in the Portuguese Chapel, first in the Musalman style by a profound reverence, then in the Christian way by kneeling in front of it, and lastly by prostrating himself, like a Hindu before an idol. Indeed, in the religion which he afterwards invented, it is possible, as I think, to trace an attempt to reconcile the conflicting claims of his queen and his conscience. But, although Christianity never won over Akbar as a convert, Queen Maria's religion yet made considerable way. Ranke mentions three princes of the Royal House who were duly baptised, and Gustave Le Bon affirms that in Jehangir's reign the number of distinguished Christians at Court was sixty. That graceless prince himself hung in his palace images of Christ and the Virgin, and in a fit of drunken expansiveness declared that Christianity was of all religions the best. For its followers were doubly blest. They were free to eat both beef and pork.

Akbar died in 1605, and from the evidence collected by Mr. Gracias, it seems probable that Maria survived him. If so we may perhaps trace to her influence two great diplomatic victories which the Portuguese gained in the early years of Jehangir's reign. The first was the reply given by the Emperor to Hawkins, the first English envoy. He came with a letter from James I, but was told in open Durbar that the great Mogal could not demean himself by corresponding with so insignificant a kinglet. The second was an offensive and defensive treaty drawn up between the delegates of the Emperor and of the Goanese Viceroy Dom Jeronymo de Azevedo. The following is a translation of the first article in the Portuguese text :—

"Seeing that the English and the Dutch come in the guise of merchants to these countries in order to settle in them and to conquer lands, because they themselves live in Europe in wretchedness and destitution; and (as) their presence in India will cause harm to all as was shown in the war which they brought about between Mogals and Portuguese (*sic*), the said delegates will agree that the King Jehangir and the Viceroy of India will not trade with the aforesaid nations nor will they be received into their harbours or sold ammunitions or anything else; first the Viceroy and his successors will be obliged to drive them from the Gujarat sea within three months of their arrival*, and if they put into the Surat harbour, the king permits the Portuguese to land the necessary cannon to defeat them and drive them away and will give the Portuguese all the help necessary to do so. And the English, who are at present in the lands and territories of the said king, will quit them, together with their factories, *via* Masulipatam."

Here we must leave Maria Mascarenhas, but even though she may have tried to further her country's interests at our expense we still owe her a deep debt of gratitude. In 1640 Alvarez, driven to despair by the Military activity of Richelieu, called out the arrièreban of Portugal and Spain. The Catalans, ever ready to rise against Castile, sprang to arms and proclaimed themselves a republic under French protection. Fired by their example, Portugal threw

* The fleets came each year with the favouring wind

off the Spanish yoke and offered her crown to John, Duke of Braganza, in whose veins flowed the blood of the old Burgundian line. Catalonia, deserted by France, had to submit. But Portugal won the English alliance and her own independence by offering with a great dowry the Princess Catherine to Charles II. Now in that dowry were included the harbour and island of Bombay, which the charms of Queen Maria had saved from the Mogal conqueror. Thus, but for her, Catherine of Braganza's dowry, must have been sought elsewhere. And the Presidency of Bombay might now be cramped within Ascension or Madeira island; or, worse still, *urbs prima in Indis* might be located in some fever-haunted swamp among the mouths of the Amazon.

THE PESHWAS OF POONA.

A Lecture Delivered at the small Memorial Hall

In chosing as my subject, the Poona Peshwas, I was chiefly guided quite apart from the local interest of the subject by the circumstance that so far in my humble opinion, sufficient justice has not been done to the achievements of this extraordinary family. There has been too great a tendency, certainly among English writers, to overlook the real change of dynasty that took place when Balaji Bajirao made his coup d'état. The first dynasty in historical Maharashtra consisted of Shivaji, his sons Shambhu and Rajaram, and Shambhu's son Shahu. The second dynasty consisted of Balaji Bajirao, Madhavrao I, Narayenrao, Madhavrao II and Bajirao Raghunathrao. These two dynasties occupied three periods. During the first of these periods the Maratha kings both reigned and ruled. During the second period, that is, during the last half of Shahu's life the Maratha kings reigned and the Peshwas ruled.. During the third period, *i.e.*, from Shahu's death to the English conquest, the Peshwas both reigned and ruled. The Maratha dynasty no doubt still survived but as State prisoners only, and exercised no more influence on the policy of Maharashtra than did the Eastern

Emperors on Italian affairs at the time of Odoacer. In the course of the lecture I have endeavoured to present before you the second dynasty as a whole. And, to do so, I have found it necessary to sketch not only the third period, but the second period also of Maratha history. From this sketch I have omitted everything that was not essential to the narrative. I have even done so at the risk of producing a mere arid and jejune string of facts. But the time at my disposals, both for preparation and for addressing you, has been so short that this was inevitable.

Let us first approach the subject with the query, what is a Peshwa ? Lord Macaulay in his essay on Warren Hastings defined him in the following words: "Peshwa or Mayor of the palace; a great hereditary magistrate, who kept a court with kingly state at Poona and whose authority was obeyed in the spacious provinces of Aurangabad and Bijapur." Now in another essay, Macaulay charged Robert Montgomery with having in one of his lines achieved the worst of all similitudes. Mr. Montgomery might possibly have retorted that his critic had achieved the worst of all definitions. The Peshwa was not a Mayor either in the literal or in the derived sense. Being a Brahmin, he was not likely to have held any high office except a priestly one in a Maratha's palace. He was not a Magistrate either hereditary or elective. Aurangabad was primarily a part of the Moglai. And the Peshwa's authority extended not merely over Bijapur but was co-extensive with the Maratha Empire. What then was a Peshwa ? The title, as the name denotes, was a Persian one and seems to have been introduced by the Bahamani kings. For Grant Duff mentions, that in 1529 A. D. Boora Khan Nizam Shah of Bijapur made a Brahmin Kavarsing a Peshwa. The title is thus very akin to the English one of Premier, which taken from the French title of premier minister, has now become an integral part of the English system of government.

The first Peshwa in Maratha times was Shamraj Pant who held that office under Shivaji in A. D. 1656. He was succeeded by Moropant Pingale who was the first among the Asht Pradhans or the King's Cabinet, and from his time onwards the Peshwa was the leading Minister of the Crown. The next question to arise is, how did the office become hereditary in one family and what was its origin? The surname of this family was Bhat, a word, which although signifying priest, had become just an ordinary family name, as we say Mr. Priest or Mr. Vicars. The father of the founder of the dynasty was one Vishvanath* Bhat who was the Deshmukh of Shriwardhan, a Konkani town near the mouth of the Savitri. He had two sons, Balaji and Janoji. On their father's death they acted as Joint Deshmukhs until the Sidi of Janjira seized Janoji, took him to Janjira, and there putting him in a sack flung him into the sea. Balaji escaped to the town of Velas where he took shelter with one Balaji Mahadev Bhanu. It was, however, impossible to remain so near to Janjira, and Bhanu, in the true spirit of friendship, left with his two brothers Hari and Ramaji to their home and accom-

* *Vide* Peshwa's Bakhar by Mr. Sane.

panied his friend to Satara. The starting of these two adventures had a great effect on the subsequent history of Maharashtra. For, one became the ancestor of the Poona Peshwas, and the other the ancestor of their greatest Minister, Nana Phadnavis.

The time they reached Satara was propitious to adventure. For Shahu, released on Aurangzeb's death, was trying to recover his kingdom from the hands of his aunt Tarabai. On Shahu's side were Khanderao Dabhade and Dhanaji Jadhav and in March, 1708, Shahu was by their aid formally installed as Maharaja Chhatrapati. Among Dhanaji's Karkuns was one Abaji Purandare * the ancestor of the noble house of that name and then Kulkarni of Saswad. To him Balaji Vishvanath attached himself and by his influence secured a post under Dhanaji Jadhav recently appointed by Shahu as Senapati or Commander-in-Chief. Balaji Vishvanath's talents soon made themselves known and Dhanaji Jadhav before his death in 1709 gave him complete control of his finances. This favour, however, almost led to Balaji's extinction. Chandrasen Jadhav, Dhanaji's son, regarded the new favourite with intense jealousy which was exasperated by Balaji's appointment by Shahu, after Dhanaji's death to check the Raja's share out of the Senapati's collections. A trifling hunting dispute served as an excuse and Balaji was, together with his two sons, forced to ride for his life to Pandugad where Chandrasen beseiged him. Fortunately for Balaji he had been at the time employed by the king. Nothing else would have saved him. As it was Shahu sent the

* Grant Duff, I, 302.

royal troops under Jadhav's rival Nimbalkar who defeated the Senapati and rescued the beseiged. Balaji now became a regular servant of the king and rapidly rose. The long regency and the endless wars had made the king's authority over his generals little more than nominal. Jadhav abandoned his service. Thorat set up as a freebooter. Angria was openly independent. The rise of Balaji, however, added the necessary vigour to restore the kingly authority. Thorat was after some difficulty captured and although Angria was at first successful, his very success ultimately caused the supremacy of Balaji. The then Peshwa was Bhairopant Pingale. To him was given the command of the expedition against Angria. He conducted it with such imbecility that his troops were completely defeated. The fort of Lohgad which commands the Bhorghat fell with the Peshwa into Angria's hands, and that daring pirate prepared, as it was believed, to march on Satara. In this supreme moment Shahu turned to Balaji Vishvanath. The latter by skilful diplomacy won over Angria, and by combining their armies in a common attack on the Sidi of Janjira stripped the latter of enough land to pay for a bribe to Angria, and thus is one campaign secured for his master a powerful ally and avenged the death of his own brother. King Shahu was overjoyed and removing Bhairu Pingale from the rank of Peshwa appointed in 1714 Balaji Vishvanath in his place. This I take it was one of the most dazzling rises in history. In 1708 he had come a homeless fugitive to a foreign land. Six years later he had become supreme in its councils.

Nor was he unworthy of his fortune. Under his guidance the uncertain policy of Shahu's early reign disappeared. His government once again reverted to the daring policy of Shivaji. The unfruitful depredations of isolated leaders gave place to a definite scheme of conquest. In fact, there came over the foreign relations of Maharashtra such a change as that which was seen in the Revolutionary Government at the advent of Bonaparte, or in Rome when the timid caution of the Senate gave place to the bold imperialism of Lucullus.

It was not long before Balaji's energy and talents obtained for his master a great reward. In A. D. 1712 Aurangzeb's son and successor Sultan Muazam died, and his grandson Farrokshiar obtained the throne. His success in doing so was chiefly due to the courage and ability of two high-born Mahomedan brothers, Abdullakhan and Hussein Ali Khan, usually known in history as the Sayads. But once on the throne the Emperor wished to destroy his allies. They in turn appealed to the Marathas and in 1718 a combined army under Balaji Vishvanath marched on Delhi. The emperor was seized and not long afterwards murdered and the Marathas obtained in 1719 a full recognition of their Swaraj over such territories as Shivaji occupied at his death and the Chauth *plus* 10 per cent. called the Sardeshmukhi on practically the whole Deccan. They seem also to have obtained the Sayads' tacit consent to levy tribute in Malwa and Gujarat.

This was the crowning achievement of this able and loyal man. He found Shahu's dominion a distracted principality. He left it a growing and vigorous empire. In the very height of his fame and in the full tide of success his frame gave way beneath the labours imposed on it. In October, 1720, he retired to Saswad where he lingered for only a few days.

About the same time there died another Maratha officer of great distinction, Khanderao Dabhade. Descended from the Mukadam of Talegaon he had earned Rajaram's gratitude by carrying him an immense distance from the besieged fort of Panala. Raised eventually to the rank of Senapati or Commander-in-Chief, he had also established himself firmly in Gujerat. His relations with Balaji Vishwanath seem to have remained friendly, but on their death there sprang up a great and fatal rivalry between their sons Trimbakrao and Bajirao. Bajirao Balaji was then in the flower of his age and had hoped, as a matter of course, to succeed his father as Peshwa. But this bold, aspiring, extremely able man met with unexpected obstacles. The speedy rise and the great talents of his father had awakened the jealousy of the local magnates. At their head was *Shriniwasrao, Pratinidhi of Aundh, a wise man and brave soldier and perhaps best known to fame as the founder of Mahuli. He strongly objected to the promotion of the young Chitpawan over the heads of the Asht Pradhans. Eventually, however, Shahu made as a kind of compromise Trimbakrao Dabhade Senapati and Bajirao Peshwa. The former at once allied himself to the old Deccan party and the rivalry of the two factions became clearly defined when Bajirao proposed to extend the Maratha con-

* Also called Shripatrao.

quest beyond Malwa into Hindustan. The Pratinidhi opposed him on the ground that it was time to consolidate the king's possessions, to restore the finances and to introduce a more careful discipline in the army. Bajirao, however, knew that such a policy would play his enemies' game. Pcace was to the advantage of the hereditary nobles with powerful local interest. War was necessary to the schemes of the brilliant adventurer, who could only maintain himself by the creation of a mercenary army and a succession of victorics. He, therefore, scoffed at the Pratinidhi's timid counsels, and asked how Shivaji would have fared had he been guided by them. He then disclosed that his policy aimed at no less than the conquest of the whole empire of the Mogals. "Strike," he cried, "strike at the trunk of the withering tree and the branches must fall of themselves." His eloquence won the day and embarked the Marathas on a vigorous policy of universal aggression.

The period was favourable to thePeshwa's schemes. The Mogal empire was reduced to a condition bordering on paralysis by the dissensions of the Emperor's ministers. The Syuds had in their turn been displaced by the Nizam-ul-mulk, a Turani Mogal of great talents and experience. He again, disgusted at the folly and the levity of the new Emperor, threw up the post of vazier to be first governor and then independent ruler of the Deccan. Bajirao sought the line of least resistance, and in 1726, invaded first Malwa and then the Carnatic as far as Seringapatam. The next year's victim was the Nizam, who, it must be admitted, deserved to the full his punishment. He tried to take advantage of the division of the Maratha empire made at Shahu's accession and set up Shambaji, the Chief of Kolhapur, as heir to the whole. Bajirao would not stoop to negotiation, and after a brilliant campaign in which the old soldier was completely out-generalled, forced him to accept most humilating terms. But here the Peshwa was obliged to halt. A new and far more formidable danger threatened him. The Deccan party led by Trimbakrao Dabhade broke into open revolt and allied themselves with the Nizam. Here again, however, Bajirao's talents triumphed. He fell on the Dhabhade's army near Dabhoi in Gujarat, and after a desperate struggle in which the Senapati perished, destroyed it. The Nizam in haste secured his safety by an agreement not to molest the future action of the Marathas, and thus opened to the Peshwa, now supreme master of Maharastra, a safe road to Delhi. Nor was Bajirao slow to take it. After a short and successful campaign against the Sidi of Janjira, the grand army under Bajirao advanced on Delhi. Close by he pitched his camp, defeated two Mogal forces and was not boght off eventually, except by a large indemnity and by the complete cession of the whole of Malwa now known as Central India. While this brilliant campaign was in progress, Bajirao's brother Chimnaji was carrying out the new policy with no less vigour to the west. The Portuguese, who for many years had had a footing on the Malabar coast, joined on account of some real or fancied grievance, the pirate Angria in an attack on Kolaba. A great Maratha army under Chimnaji hastened to the spot.

First Bandra and Salsette fell, and then, after a furious seige, the Portuguese were compelled to surrender Bassein, and the whole seaboard of the Northern Konkan was added to the rapidly-growing Maratha possessions. To the cession of Malwa, however, the Nizam objected and once again he and Bajirao appeared on opposite sides. The latter after two successful campaigns found at last that his resources were unequal to the subjugation of the Deccan. The third campaign ended undecisively, and Bajirao overwhelmed with debt, harassed by disease and in despair at this check to the progress of his schemes hoped to recoup himself by another successful war in Hindustan. Death, however, overtook him on the banks of the Narbudda where he died on the 28th Apirl, 1740. He had been for 20 years Peshwa, and if his policy had been of the too forward kind he yet had achieved brilliant things. He had made himself, with hardly the exception of the king, the supreme master of the State. He had fought with success the greatest soldiers in India, and if he met with a check in the end it was perhaps because, as Shriniwasrao had indicated, consolidation should have preceded conquest. His character is perhaps best indicated by a story told in the Peshwa's Bakhar. The Emperor wished to know what manner of man it was who led from Satara armies to threaten the august throne of Delhi, so he sent a painter to depict him as he happened first to see him The painter found Bajirao on horseback with his spear slung carelessly over his shoulder. As he went he picked the ears of corn and unhusked them between his hands and ate them. In this position the painter drew him and shewed his picture to the Emperor. The latter looked at it and said "*wuh shaitan hai*," and gave the order "*Baji Rao, yanshi samjoot padoon wates lavle pahije*."*

The firm hold that the Bhat family had taken in the Satara State is well exemplified by the circumstance that Bajirao's son Balaji succeeded him as Peshwa without serious opposition. But it was not long before the Dabhade faction raised up a new enemy in Raghuji Bhosle. This person, the founder of the afterwards famous house of Nagpur, had obtained Shahu's favour by his skill as a hunter and sealed it by his marriage with the sister of Shahu's wife Sakvarbai. The subject of the dispute was Raghoji's claim to levy independent tribute in Bengal. Balaji took the field and proved himself, like his father and grandfather, a skilful general. Raghuji was defeated, and the new Peshwa attempted to make surer foundations for the Kingdom. From 1746 to 1749 he devoted himself to improving the revenue system and encouraging agriculture. But towards the end of 1749 it was clear that King Shahu's long reign was coming to a close. He had no son and had refused to adopt one, due, it is believed, to his knowledge that his nephew Ram Raja was alive.

Sakvarbai, Shahu's wife, was bitterly hostile to the Peshwa's domination. The crisis was therefore imminent. Balaji met it with resolution and skill. He surrounded Satara with 30,000 men, and on the morning that Shahu died surprised and imprisoned all the members of his family. Sakvarbai, his enemy,

---

He is a devil. Make terms with him and get rid of him.

was forced to commit sati. Ram Raja was imprisoned and the capital was transferred from Satara to Poona. In that town Bajirao had already established himself in the fortified palace still named Shanwar Wada. Two stories are told to account for his choice. One is that he saw a dog being pursued by a hare and so assumed that the dwellers on that spot were invincible. The other is that his horse stumbled and from it he argued that it was intended by Providence that he should remain there. A more probable reason was the favourable situation of Poona, sheltered alike by Singhad and Purandhar, the latter of which had been in the private possession of the Bhats since the time of Balaji Vishvanath.

From this date 1750 A. D. the Peshwas became ruling princes and it remains for us to see how they acquitted themselves of their new duties. Had but ordinary good fortune waited on them the new masters of Maharashtra would have been equal to the situation. But a fresh and formidable peril was threatening India. In the winter of 1747-48 Ahmedshah Abdalli, a prince of Herat and an old soldier of Nadir Shah, had begun a series of incursions across the North-West frontier. The Delhi empire which had received a fatal blow during the invasion of Nadir Shah in 1739 was helpless. The matter eventually became so pressing that in 1757 the Peshwa's brother Ragunathrao led a large Maratha army to oppose the Afghans. Raghunathrao had more than a full share of his illustrious father's generalship and without difficulty drove the Afghans across the mountains. Unfortunately the profits of the expedition were far less than its cost and Chimnaji's son

Sadashivrao, the Peshwa's first cousin and favourite, a man of great financial and administrative talents, gratified his jealousy of Raghunathrao and made so much of the latter's alleged mismanagement that he at last succeeded in himself superseding him. The change was disastrous. Ahmed Shah, who would have found Raghunathrao probably more than a match, outmanoeuvred Sadashivrao, hemmed him in and eventually utterly destroyed him, the heir apparent Vishvas Rao and the Grand Army of the Marathas. The disaster was too much for the Peshwa, who lingered but a short time after he learnt the news and died among the temples on Parvati Hill.

As Vishvas Rao had fallen, the next heir was Balaji's second son Madhavrao. His task was a colossalone. Ahmed Shah was master of Hindustan. The Nizam was combining with Jankoji Jadhav to overthrow the Peshwa Government in favour of the old Maratha line. The treasury was empty. There was no army and Raghunathrao was openly anxious to secure for himself the Peshwai. All these difficulties had to be faced by a boy of sixteen. Yet the great house that had already produced Balaji Vishvanath, Bajirao I, Balaji II, and Chimnaji was not yet exhausted and the abilities and spirit of Madhavrao proved as great as any of his predecessors. Raghunathrao was conciliated. The Nizam was signally defeated at Rakshabhuvan. Ahmed Shah recrossed the Afghan frontier. One great force under the Peshwa in person advance as far as Seringapatam. Another Maratha army crossed the Chambal, looted Rohilkhand, and encamped at

Delhi. By a most unlucky chance, however, this gallant prince had contracted consumption and just when his government was threatening to over run all India he died aged only 28 at Theur. As Grant Duff very justly observed, "The plains of Panipat were not more fatal to the Maratha empire, than the early end of this excellent prince." We have now, gentlemen, passed the apogee of the greatness of the Peshwas. I shall shortly as possible accompany you to their melancholy fall. Madhavrao's younger brother Narain Rao was duly installed, but Raghunathrao first reconciled to and then interned by Madhavrao, again aspired to the Peshwaship. Narain Rao was brutally murdered in his palace by the guards, and another young Prince for whom shrewd observers had prophesied a great future was lost to the Maratha empire. Raghunathrao, however, again failed to secure his object. An enquiry held by Ram Shastri revealed that he had connived if not at the murder at the attack and it being shortly afterwards discovered that Narain Rao's widow Gangabai was pregnant a regency government was carried on in her name by the ministers among whom were Sakharam Bapu and the descendent of Balaji Vishvanath's friend Bhanu, now famous as Nana Phadnavis. On the 18th April, 1774, Gangabai gave birth to a son Madhavrao II. This put an end to Raghunathrao's hopes. He, however, struggled unceasingly against his grand nephew's dominion He first collected 30,000 men from Shinde and Holkar and then induced the Bombay Government to lend him their active support. In this way began what is known in English history as the First Maratha

War. A joint English and rebel force advanced from Gujarat and defeated the Poona army at Arras. The war was, however, stopped by Warren Hastings from Calcutta before it reached any decisive stage. Raghunathrao, however, in the cold weather of 1779, induced the Bombay Government again to assist him. But this time the regency were able to repel the danger. The English were defeated at Wadgaon, but assistance arriving from Calcutta, they overran Bassein and a large part of the Konkan. Goddard was, however, repulsed near Panwel and the regency and the English eventually made a treaty on the *status quo ante* basis. Raghunathrao, the cause of the trouble, received a handsome pension and died in 1784, leaving two sons, Bajirao and Chimnaji Appa. For the next eleven years Nana Phadnavis conducted the government. I do not propose here to detail to you with what skill he did so. Enemies were rising up on many sides. A soldier of fortune, Haidar Ali, had established and bequeathed a powerful kingdom to his son. Shinde had half thrown off his allegiance and disputed Nana Phadnavis' preeminence. The English power was rapidly growing both in the south and the west. Nevertheless, Nana Phadnavis struggled desperately and on the whole successfully to check the decline of Maharashtra. Unfortunately, the effects of the Civil War were not easily to be effaced. Many of Raghunathrao's adherents still lived and they, as well as many others, sympathised not only with the lot of his son Bajirao but also with the growing Madhavrao, whom Nana Phadnavis as well kept under jealous supervision. It is probable that the old man had no other object but the young man's good, and had but forgotten that the years, which passed quickly over his own head were, creating an immense change in the young prince. A secret correspondence sprang up between the two cousins, Madhavrao and Bajirao, whose situations were in many respects so similar.* It was discovered by the great Minister, and his anger was so terrible that Madhavrao, broken hearted by his reproaches, threw himself from an upper storey in the palace into the court-yard round which now cluster the Courts of the Poona Sub-Judges. On his death bed he expressed a wish that Bajirao should succeed him, and after a series of deep intrigues Bajirao did obtain the Masnad which his father had failed so often to secure. The new prince's first efforts were directed towards destroying such of his friends as had helped him to rise. Nana Phadnavis, now full of years, was treacherously seized, and an attempt was made to seize Shinde in open Darbar which would certainly have succeeded had not Bajirao's heart failed him. The intentions of Bajirao became, however, known to their would-be-victim, and their discovery naturally estranged all the great Jahagirdars. The estrangement led to an absolute disregard for the Peshwa's supremacy. On Tukoji Holkar's death Shinde seized on the Holkar's estates. Yeshwantrao Holkar, an illegitimate son took the field in the old Maratha fashion. Eventually, the two feudatories fought near Hadapsar and Yeshwantrao Holkar was completely victorious. The Peshwa, who had latterly been friendly to Shinde, fled

* They were both closely watched. I should, however, say here that recent researches brought to my notice by Mr. Dravid, editor of the "Dnyan Prakash," make it doubtful whether Madhavrao's death was not accidental.

to Bombay, and the victorious Holkar thoroughly plundered the inhabitants of the beautiful capital. The Peshwa to obtain revenge agreed to the treaty of Bassein.

In return for English assistance he promised to maintain a large body of hired troops, and signed his own complete political subordination. Amritrao, his elder adopted brother, had, however, in the meantime usurped the Peshwai, and the interference of the British brought on them the whole confederacy of the Maratha Empire. The great resources, however, which that Government had then acquired, and the ability of the two brothers, the Marquis and General Wellesley, then at the head of the Civil and Military Government, enabled the British to restore Bajirao. Shinde was defeated at Assaye and Laswari, Raghoji Bhosle at Argano, and Holkar, after some brilliant initial successes ,was driven out of the Deccan. Bajirao had obtained a signal revenge, but at a high, and as he soon came to think, at a too high price. Quarrels arose between the allies and they came to a head over the question of the arrest of Trimbakji Dengale, the murderer of the Gaikwad's minister Gangadhar Shastri. Eventually, Bajirao was forced to sign the treaty of Poona which placed him still more under English protection. Bajirao, however, had no intention of adhering to it. He secretly enrolled a quantity of troops, and hoped by taking the initiative to gain such successes against the English as would bring to his aid the great Maratha Jahagirdars. The successes, however, never came. His troops were defeated in every battle and he himself eventually surrendered on the 3rd June, 1818, to

Sir John Malcolm. He was allowed the handsome pension of 8 lacs a year. He retired to Bithur near Cawnpore where he lived for nearly 30 years, dying eventually on the 28th January, 1851.

With the English conquest, the line of Peshwas came, of course, to an end, and I may, perhaps, be permitted to enquire, what was the reason of their complete collapse ? Many different causes have been assigned to it,—Western aggression, the independent attitude of the feudatories, the battle of Panipat. These all, no doubt, contributed to the downfall, but in my humble judgment were symptoms of the disease rather than the disease itself. The evil lay deeper. In his "Decline and Fall", Gibbon has observed that Asiatic monarchy is an unceasing round of valour, greatness, degeneracy and decay. This remark is singularly untrue, of some, at any rate, of the native Indian kingdoms. The august dynasty of Udaipur, which still ranks so high among the principalities of India, was hoary with age when the Catholic Church was founded and of respectable antiquity when Sophocles was writing tragedies and Pericles dallying with Aspasia. But the remark is true both of Eastern and Western usurpers. And in spite of their great services, usurpers the Peshwas were always regarded by the great body of Maharashtra. Had the Peshwas been able to extinguish and not merely intern the successors of Shahu, they would, no doubt, have in the end been regarded as legitimate monarchs. But public opinion was too strong for them. They never dared lay sacrilegious hands on the descendants of Shivaji Bhosle. And, indeed, there is no more marvellous achievement of that Titanic figure than that during $1\frac{1}{2}$ centuries his memory, the mere terror of his name was sufficient to protect his helpless posterity. Now as they were usurpers, the Peshwas' kingdom was subject to the common rule. Decay was the inevitable accompaniment of their deterioration. During the Peshwas' greatness, Western aggression was promptly dealt with. The Portuguese were, as we have seen, driven out of Bassein, and it is idle to argue that the English could not have been similarly overpowered. The independence of the Jahagirdars was a still later symptom. The great Mahadji Shinde himself had tried to measure himself against the first Madhavrao, but the young prince drove him from his presence completely cowed. And what was the battle of Panipat, but the result of Balaji Bajirao's weak yielding to the jealous clamour of his favourite cousin ? Had his strength been still unimpaired, Raghunathrao would have been retained at the head of the army, and there would have been no disaster. But the weakness of the Central Government began in the closing years of Balaji's reign and succeeding Peshwas were never able completely to cure the disease. In Madhvarao's reign it might have been got under had he only lived longer or executed Raghunathrao. His early death ruined the central Government, for the regency were unable to restore health to it. Finally when Bajirao succeeded the disease had got completely the upper hand. The Maratha empire was already doomed. He but hastened the end.

I have now come to the end of my lecture. I must thank you for the attention and kindness with which you have listened to me. But before I conclude

I would make of you an earnest request. The subject which I have discussed is an extremely delicate one. I have endeavoured to eliminate from it all matters in the least likely to give offence. It is, however, possible that being a foreigner, I may have quite unintentionally wounded some sensibilities. Should I have done so I would only ask that no ill motive may be imputedto me and that as the intention was absent it may be judged that I have committed no offence. On the other hand, I shall be deeply gratified if I have succeeded in giving you even a momentary glimpse of any single member of the great house that turned the little township of Poona into a mighty and beautiful metropolis—of Balaji Vishvanath, the wise progenitor, Bajirao I, the orator and soldier whose fiery imagination like the gate of the Shanwar Wada looked ever towards the golden throne of Delhi; Balaji Vishvanath, the bold but unfortunate usurper; Madhavrao I, the most brilliant perhaps of all, whom death snatched away in his glorious prime; Narayanrao and Madhavrao II, killed on the very threshold of manhood, and last of all Bajirao II, gayest, handsomest but, alas, most incapable of princes.

IN THE COURT OF THE YOUNGER MADHAVRAO.*

It used to be some years ago—and I daresay that it still is—a not uncommon saying that Hindu writers have no historical sense, and it must be admitted that the earlier literature of India afforded some ground for this reproach. It was left to three Englishmen, Colonel Tod, Mr. Forbes and Captain Grant Duff, to write the histories of Rajasthan, Kathiavad and the Maharashtra. The splendid period of Mussulman greatness found no Hindu historian and even the spirited bakhars of the great Deccan houses can hardly be termed, in the usual sense of the word, histories. But whatever may formerly have been the case, to-day the censure is no longer deserved. In "Karan Ghelo" a Gujarati author has written the finest historical novel produced in either hemisphere since Dumas wrote the wondrous tale of "The Three Musketeers." And of recent years the Deccan has furnished historical novelists like Mr. Hari Apte and historians like Mr. Dattatraya Parasnis. It is with the most recent work of the latter author that the present article deals. And the book has a double interest, for throughout its pages may be seen side by side old-fashioned and modern Marathi. The former in the letters of

---

* Savai Madhavrao Peshvayancha Darbar. By Mr. D. B. Parasnis rinted at the Nirnayasagara Press, Poona.

Nana Phadnavis and his agents is crabbed, ambiguous, often unintelligible. The latter wielded by Mr. Parasnis' admirable pen is clear, vigorous, and so permeated with Western thought that sentence after sentence might almost be literally translated into English.

To return, however, to my subject. In his latest book, "The Court of the Younger Madhavrao," Mr. Parasnis has written of the establishment of the first permanent English embassy at the Court of Poona. There had been no doubt several earlier English envoys. As long ago as 1674 A.D. Sir Henry Oxenden and Dr. Fryer had visited Shivaji at Raigad. Then in 1739 Captain Gordon had been to see King Shahu at Satara. In 1759 William Price had treated with the Third Peshwa, Balaji Bajirao. In 1767 Mostyn had visited Madhavrao I, and in 1776 Colonel Upton had brought to a succesful close the negotiations leading to the treaty of Purandhar. But these were all transitory visits, and the East India Company had long felt the need of some permanent responsible medium through whom they might both acquire and impart information. After the disastrous campaign of Wadgaon, the Company had, through a sense of gratitude to Mahadji Shinde for his treatment of their troops,employed him as their intermediary. But it was not long before this method proved unsatisfactory. Shinde's thoughts were directed towards Delhi rather than Poona, and it was impossible that one so deeply engaged in Hindustani affairs could spare the time or trouble to be a successful agent of the Company. After considerable hesitation and after long discussion with the

Calcutta Government, it was decided that a Bombay officer should be selected, but that he should represent not Bombay but the Governor-General. The next step was to obtain the consent of the Poona Court. This was no easy matter. The continual presence of an English envoy might be construed as a sign of inferiority which the Maratha Government were naturally loth to admit. The meridian of their glory had no doubt passed, but although the evening shadows were soon to fall the setting sun for the time shone brightly enough. The terrible calamity of Panipat had been in a measure repaired by the elder Madhavrao, and the spoils of Hyderabad and the Carnatic had replenished the empty treasury. The civil campaigns against Raghunathrao had indeed shaken the structure of the empire, but the ability of the regent Nana Phadnavis coped with each new difficulty as it came. The English were by the treaty of Salbai induced to abandon Raghunathrao, and if victory had not as of old followed the Yellow Banner yet in two campaigns the English had wrested nothing from the Poona Court. On the whole, it was a fair time for Maharashtra. The reforms initiated by Balaji Bajirao revised by Madhavrao the First and still further developed by the regent had rendered the lot of the Deccan peasant by no means unenviable. Trade, no doubt, stagnated, but there was vast wealth stored in the houses of the Maratha nobles. Civil talents found an opening in Nana Phadnavis' administration and in Malwa where the wide lands of the Holkar Shahi were guarded the virtues and wisdom of Ahilyabai. Nor were adventures lacking to the adventurous. Raids were in constant progress into the Carnatic or the Moglai; and far away at Ujjain were forming beneath the eagle eyes of De Boigne those renowned brigades, who, many years later, though deserted by their leaders, yet faced Lake's attack with unfaltering courage; who burst like a flood over Upper India; who broke in pieces the old thrones of Rajasthan, and who accomplished what five centuries of Mussulman invaders had failed to achieve, for they humbled to the very dust the lordly pride of Mewar.

What than in the end induced Nana Phadnavis to consent to the English proposal? There can be little doubt that it was the growing menace of Tipu Sultan's kingdom. His father Haidar Ali had no doubt been on the whole hostile to the English, but he had been no less so to the Marathas, and it would not have been difficult for the Company to induce Tipu Sultan to join in a league against the Poona Government which. pressed on both sides, would have found it a hard task to resist. So to prevent what he most feared, an alliance of the English with Tipu, Nana Phadnavis agreed reluctantly to a permanent English envoy at the Peshwa's Court. There was yet another step to be taken, and that was to induce, without offending him, Mahadji Shinde to relinquish his post as intermediary between the English and the Peshwa. This delicate task was entrusted to the hero of Mr. Parasnis' work, Charles Warre Malet. This remarkable man came of an obscure English family. His father was a poor country parson who found it difficult no his small income to bring up his children. Thus when his son Charles, born in A. D. 1752, reached the age of eighteen, his father gladly accepted on his behalf a writership in the East India Company. In the winter of 1770 the young man landed in Bombay, and his earlier service was spent in Muscat, Bushire and in other coast towns along the Persian Gulf. In 1774, he was selected to officiate as English Agent at the Court of Cambay. Here he earned the approval of his chiefs by an act of resolution certainly remarkably in a boy of twenty-three. When the intense feeling roused by the murder of Narain Rao had alienated from Raghunathrao the great jaghirdars, he turned in despair to the English with whom, on March 6th, 1775, he drew up a treaty making to them large cessions in the Konkan in return for the support of their troops. Before, however, these could reach him he was surprised and signally defeated near the Mahi river by the regent's army. He fled with only 1,000 horses to Cambay where the Nawab was unwilling to receive him. But the young English envoy, although he knew nothing of the treaty, insisted on sheltering him and enabled him to embark *via* Bhavnagar in safety for Bombay. The grateful pretender, in a letter quoted by Mr. Parasnis, exclaimed : "You did more for me than my father Bajirao. He gave me my life but you not only saved it, but my honour as well !" The Bombay Government showed their appreciation by confirming Malet at Cambay where he seems to have remained until 1785, when they were asked by Calcutta to choose a representative for the Poona Court. Before this could be done Shinde's consent had, as I have said, to be obtained and Malet was selected for this delicate mission. Going by sea from Bombay to Surat, Malet marched from there to Ujjain. There he met Mahadji Shinde. The difficulties were great for, as intermediary between the English and the Peshwa, Shinde retained an effective control over affairs at Poona. Nevertheless Malet induced the reluctant prince to write that if the Peshwa had no objection to the new embassy, he had none. A yet greater triumph was in store for the young civil servant. For, on his return to Bombay, he learnt that Shinde had privately written to Governor Boddom that, should the Peshwa consent, Shinde hoped that Mr. Malet might be chosen as envoy.

His wish was granted, for the Peshwa had already consented and Malet started for Poona. The following letter, written on the 11th February, 1786, by Bahirav Raghunath to Nana Phadnavis reports Malet's slow advance, and its closing sentence shows that our countryman, distinguished though he was, was not above certain deplorable frailties.

"You ordered me to report, when Mr. Malet "left Bombay, how far he had gone and when he "would reach Poona. Accordingly (I inform you "that) he reached Panwell on the 12th instant. "(Hindu month). He remained for eight days "there. On the 21st he left, and I was informed by "letter that on the 22nd he had come to Khalapur "near Khopvali just below the Ghats. The "following day he was to climb them. He will "remain two days at Khandala. The reason why "his marches are so slow is because he requires "labourers for no less than 500 to 700 head-loads. "This leads to confusion and waste of time. ". . . With him are the following:—Six topi-

"walas* including Malet himself. Of these, three "of them are entitled to palanquins. There are "35 horses, 200 guards, 100 servants, 50 kamathi "porters, 75 palanquin men, 425 Mhars, 2 elephants, "4 palanquins. His camp kit consists of 1 big and "2 small tents, 3 big raotis and pals for servants. "Malet's Musalman dancing girl is for also with "them in a palkhi."

On Malet's arrival at Poona there occurred a difference between him and the regent. The latter was engaged in an expedition in the Carnatic and wished Malet without delay to join his army. Malet pleaded that he wished first to pay his respects to the young Peshwa and this the regent was at last forced to allow. Malet's stay gave rise to the question where he was to stay, and his place of residence gave Bahirav Raghunath who had been entrusted with his entertainment considerable trouble. On the 4th March, 1786, he wrote as follows to Nana :—

"I have prepared a place in the Gaikwad's "houses. But he (Malet) want a roomy spot "surrounded by trees. He has, therefore, pitched "his tents opposite Parvati in the mango grove "near Anandrao Jivaji's garden. He has placed "his zanankhana"—presumably his Musalman Herodias—" inside the Gaikwad's house, but he " himself remains outside."

Although Mr. Malet was not very satisfied with this arrangement and seems to have grumbled a good

* The names applied to Englishmen by Indians are many and various. The following I have myself either heard or read :—Roumi, Feringhi, or Feranghi, Ingrej, Anrej, Angal, Mleccha, Yavan, topiwala and Janglo. The term sahiblog is within my experience only used when an Englishman is within hearing or by the servant class.

deal, his attention was soon diverted to a further question. Having gained his point and obtained leave to see the Peshwa, he had next to see that he should be properly received. He had brought with him a quantity of presents, of which one seems to have been a young ostrich. Of this Bahiravpant wrote :

"Malet has brought a shahamrag (griffin) from "Abyssinia to give to the Peshwa. It, however, "died in its cage below the Ghats. But he had its "body carried after him. The bird was very large, "being four feet high. He brought it because it "was very rare, but it is dead." The other offerings, however, remained and a heated controversy arose as to how the Peshwa should receive the envoy. Nana Phadnavis ordered that he should be given the same honours as Mr. Mostyn and Colonel Upton. Mr. Malet contended that they had merely represented the Bombay Government and that as he was the ambassador of Calcutta, he should receive the same honours as the Calcutta envoy when visiting Shinde or the Mogal. A most amusing correspondence ensued between Bahiravpant and the regent in which the former recited all the devices vainly employed to induce Malet to accept Nana Phadnavis' ruling. Eventually, it was arranged that the official reception should stand over until Malet's return from the regents camp. Malet, whom Bahiravpant described as extremely "grieved, vexed, and annoyed," was to see the Peshwa privately. An account of this interview is to be found in a letter of Janardhan Apaji to Nana Phadnavis, dated 5th March, 1786.

"To-day he (Malet) went to pay his respects to the "Peshwa. It was arranged that he should arrive "first and the Peshwa later. At the time of departure the Peshwa was to rise first so that there "should be no difficulty on the score of etiquette. "As Bahiravpant suggested and Malet insisted that "on arrival he should merely place his hand within "the Peshwa's, the latter received him unattended."*

After thus paying his respects to Madhavrao II, Mr. Malet had to join Phadnavis' army and on the 20th May, 1786, was presented at the storming of Badami. Upon this success, the Maratha forces returned to Poona where Malet began to unfold the design of the Company. This was no less than the formation of a triple alliance between the Nizam, the Marathas and the English against Mysore. As Mr. Parasnis has very justly observed, it is extraordinary that the regent should ever have joined such a scheme. Fear a league between the English and Tipu Sultan though he might, it was yet scarcely conceivable that he should play into the former's hands by joining with them against their most serious enemy. That Malet should have overcome Nana's reluctance is the highest proof of the Englishman's talents. The Nizam was similarly won over by Sir John Kennaway and eventually the representatives of all three powers formally agreed jointly to invade Mysore. The opening passage of the treaty frankly confesses its object :—

"All the three powers have treaties with Tipu. "But he has harassed all three of us. Therefore,

* The ordinary Indian salutation would have been a 'namaskar' or profound bow accompanied by on upward motion of the hands clasped in front.

"the three Governments will jointly make an "expedition and give him such punishment that "he will not have the means of harassing any of "them again." Each power was to put 25,000 men into the field and the Nizam was to employ the two Company's regiments in his service. Similarly two Company's regiments were to be hired to the Peshwa, if required, at the same rate of pay. The English took the field at the appointed time, but soon found that their allies were not so ready to act up to their agreement. Malet, at last, exasperated by what he thought was the regent's duplicity but what Mr. Parasnis believes to have been his lack of means, spoke to him so sharply that he directed the Maratha agent with the English army, Haripant Phadke, to ask for Malet's recall. Haripant, however, knew no English. The English General knew no Marathi. Mr. Cherry, the English interpreter, was Malet's personal friend, so Haripant had to write to Nana that under the circumstances he could not well raise the question. Eventually, Malet and Kennaway did infuse some energy into the Hyderabad and Poona administrations and the first Mysore war terminated with the humiliation of Tipu and a partition between the allies of half his kingdom, including Coorg. The East India Company, delighted with Malet's success, got the English Ministry to create him a baronet. But the regent's feelings were very different. Malet on behalf of the Company presented his bill for their regiments at the rate of Rs. 64,000 a month, *plus* Rs. 68,000 for equipment, Rs. 14,000 for transport and Rs. 40,000 as a gratuity for their gallantry. In all the bill came to Rs. 751,666. It was paid, but Nana Phadnavis in the bitterness of his heart wrote to Govindrao Kale, the Maratha envoy at Hyderabad, as follows:—

"Malet at Poona, Kinvi (Kennaway) at Hyderabad have sat down and done nothing, but have spent lakhs of rupees. While they were sitting down people said they cannot really be doing nothing, they must be devising some cunning plot. And that is what has actually happened. Now whether we like it or not we have to agree to what they say and act up to the treaty. It is true that its terms were that when Dassara came we were to send a considerable force. Dassara passed by and Diwali came and what was done was done after Diwali. (They consider) each day as if it was a yuga (age). You will say that Diwali is the same as Dassara. Pagriwalas will agree with you, but topiwalas will not be put off like that. They will take a pair of scales and they will sit down and weigh the meaning of each phrase in the treaty and they will not let you speak a single word. (They. will exclaim) 'You made a fine display! Without any trouble you have got forts and strongholds while we worked ourselves to death!' And they will certainly say that the Company has been ruined and ask how we can have the face to claim our share. I have no doubt about it. And while speaking they will roll their eyes in anger and forget all that we have done for them.'

Nor was Govindrao Kale's answer less pathetic: "The present days are very hard. At Poona you have Malet. Here we have Kinvi (Kennaway).

"They are both skilled in their work and servants "of the same master Malet writes to Kinvi what "goes on at Poona; Kinvi writes to Malet what "goes on here. Then Malet questions you and "Kinvi me and they make us answer. And this "exposes us to great bother and difficulty. They "search out whether our answers are true or false. "And the man who gets caught between them "suffers sore trouble."

In spite of Phadnavis' fears the English gave the Marathas their fair share and Malet in the end gained to some extent the regent's respect. He was even more successful with the young Peshwa whose affections as well as those of the Poona people he seems to have completely captured. In this he derived great help from Drs. Crusoe and Findley, members of his staff. They were skilful surgeons and attended on all, high or low, who needed their services. Still greater aid was given to Malet by a Mr. Wales, R. A., who visited Poona about this time, and whose skill as a portrait painter both helped his country and brought considerable profit to himself. During the five or six years he remained at Poona, he sketched all the leading men of that day, and his portrait of the regents, and of the younger Madhavrao may still be seen at Ganeshkhind. At Malet's suggestion Wales founded an art school and one of his pupils, Gangaram Tambat, made a painting of Verul caves which in 1794 was sent by Malet as a present to Sir John Shore, then Governor-General. Wales died on the 13th November, 1795, and five years later his eldest daughter Susan became Lady Malet. Surgery and painting were, however, not the only arts which the English envoy introduced. He sent for a watchmaker from Europe and microscopes, globes, and telescopes to the Peshwa and his Sardars. Nor were his gifts confined to these. For when one Mahadji Chintaman was suffering from a pain in the abdomen, Malets, gave him Rs. 125, with which to pay some Brahmins to do pradakshina* round the idol of Shri Narayan.

One of the most interesting chapters in Mr. Parasnis' book contains the account of Malet's visit to Mahableshwar in 1791 more than thirty years before those of its reputed discoverers Lodwick and Malcolm. The Peshwa, who loved Malet's society, had taken him there with him. Nana Phadnavis, however, was afraid that on the return journey the Englishman might at Satara weave an intrigue with the imprisoned Maharaja, and, as may be seen from the following letter, took steps to prevent their meeting :—

"The Peshwa and his retinue came to Wai and "after the eclipse on the 3rd Ashwin Wad went "to Mahableshwar and returned on the 4th, Malet "with him. He always goes 4 or 5 kos daily in "search of sport. There are many forts here and "he examines them daily through a telescope. "He then makes maps of them. The Maharajah, "the Queen Mother and the Satara notables sent a "message inviting the Peshwa, as he had climed "the Salpe ghat, to pay his respects to the Maha-"raja. If the Peshwa were to go Malet would accom-"pany him. Now Satara is the most important

* The pradakshina is the circling of the suppliant round the shrine with his left arm outwards. The right side of the body must be kept turned towards the idol.

"place (in the kingdom). It would be quite different "if he saw it close. So it was decided that the "Peshwa should pay his respects alone and by putting off Malet's visits from day to day the Maharaja was induced to believe that he was not coming. "So he and the Peshwa exchanged presents of "clothes, an elephant and a horse. The following "day the Peshwa and his suite returned to Wai." Nana Phadnavis thus thought that he had outwitted the envoy, but he was afterwards disgusted to learn that on the day of the Peshwa's visit to Satara fort Malet had climbed the fort of Sonjai and had observed the whole scene through a telescope.

If, however, the old regent never wholly overcame his suspicion, elsewhere Malet attained a degree of intimacy with the Poona aristocracy which, as Mr. Parasnis has observed, is extraordinary in the light of modern manners. No marriage or thread-ceremony seems to have been complete without him. He attended regularly the Ganpati festival both in the palace of the Peshwas and of the Phadkes, and Brahmins of every degree were willing to drink medicines prepared either by him or his doctors. He was, in fact, the great social success of Poona society. In 1795 the young Peshwa either threw himself or fell from the upper storey of the Shanwar Wada and after innumerable plots and counterplots his cousin Bajirao succeeded him on the royal cushion. He too came under the wand of the magician. For when Malet retired in March, 1797, the new Peshwa parted with him with the utmost reluctance and sent by him to the English King a flattering letter, in which

Malet's services were highly appreciated, and presents worth Rs. 20,000.

On his return to England Malet resided until his death in 1815 at Wilbury House. By Susan Lady Malet, he had 8 sons of whom the eldest Sir Alexander Malet succeeded to his father's title and from 1856 to 1866 was English ambassador at Berlin. Another son, Sir Arthur Malet, became a member of the Bombay Government. And a third son, Mr. Hugh Malet, while Collector of Thana, discovered by an unconscious atavism the hill station of Matheran.

Here I must take leave of Mr. Parasnis and his most interesting book. In it he has given us, sketched both in pen and pencil, the portraits of the versatile and able men who adorned the Court of the last Peshwa but one who ruled in Poona. There may be seen the dark and brooding brow of the great Nana Phadnavis who strove all in vain to pilot the ship of state through the raging waters. There too laughs at us, in the joy of his twenty years, the younger Madhavrao, all unconscious of a future terrible and untimely death. And right through the book there strides the burly figure of the English envoy, adroit, fearless, resourceful and insinuating—the stormy petrel whose presence more clearly than aught else fore the told to discerning observer the cyclone that was soon to sweep away for ever the whole structure of the Peshwa's dominion.

A MARATHI COMEDY.

A Woman's Revolt.

There are in the heart of Poona city several theatres where night after night Marathi plays are performed to Indian audiences; but into which an Englishman rarely finds his way. Should he do so, it may be that he will be well rewarded. A few weeks ago this way my own good fortune. I witnessed a play or rather part of play a evidently based on Tennyson's "Princess." The old Latin tag that "art is long and life is short" applies however, with peculiar force to Marathi dramas. The Indian, who has paid 4 annas for a seat, expects entertainment for at least an equal number of hours, so after witnessing an act or two of the play in the theatre I was forced to read the rest of it in my study.

The dramatist, Mr. Khandilkar, following the usual Marathi tradition, has taken as the time of his play the epic period of Indian history. There are advantages about this method as girls where then married at an age when they could fall in love. It is, therefore, possible to put love scenes on the stage. The chief demerit is that characters, 4,000 years old, are made to talk like Poona gentlemen of to-day, and we therefore are faced with an anachronism similar to that with which Macaulay charged Racine—"the sentiments and phrases of Versailles in the camp of Aulis." The date when "A Womans'

Revolt," as Mr. Khadilkar's play is called, opens, is shortly after the great battle of Kurukshetra. The Pandav brothers, after the twelve years of exile and one of disguise forced on them by Yudhishthira's dicing match, had at last come into their own. Their cousin Duryodhan was dead, his father King Dhritrashtra was their prisoner. Yudhishthira had ascended the throne of Hastinapura and had sent Arjuna with the Ashwamedha horse that he might exact tribute and submission wherever it roamed. Arjuna had been a year absent, and everywhere the horse had wandered, Yudhishthira had been acknowledged emperor; when in a small Himalayan kingdom it was seized and tribute was refused. The ruler Shvetketu, Tennyson's King Gama, himself acknowledged Yudhishthira's overlordship, but his daughter Pramila, going further than the Princess Ida, had established not merely a girl's college but a woman's kingdom. No man, except with letters from Shvetketu, could enter it save on pain of death and she and her female bands were prepared to resist all men's claims for superiority, including Yudhishthira's. Like King Gama, Shvetketu had not much sympathy with his daughter's views and promised Arjuna her hand if he could cure her of her folly. That invincible warrior, however, could not stain his arms with the blood of the fair sex. So it was agreed that like the Prince Florian and Cyril, he and some companions should enter Pramila's domain, and if possible, win the heart of the Princess. Arjuna took three companions, Pushpadhanwa, his commander-in-chief, a young hero who in youth had been betrothed to Pramila's commander-in-chief Rupmaya, and two old men Maitraya and Jagruka, who furnish most of the comic element in the play. They do not, like Tennyson's gallants, adopt women's disguises, but Arjuna affects to be a vakil come with an offer of marriage from Arjuna. Pushpadhanwa puts on an old man's wig and beard and pretends to be like Maitraya and Jagruka, an ancient counsellor in attendance on Arjuna's vakil. The first scene closes as the four start on their quest armed with letters from King Shvetketu. The second scene opens on the frontier of Queen Pramila's Kingdom. Some lady soldiers are on duty and are passing their time abusing the male sex when they espy Arjuna and his three attendants. They are arrested, but as they produce King Shvetketu's letters, they are brought into the Darbar of Queen Pramila and her aunt Satyamaya. The latter has the title of Guru Maharaj and she is our old friend the Lady Blanche who

> "Of faded form and haughtiest lineaments
> "With all her autumn tresses falsely brown
> "Shot side long daggers at us, a tiger cat
> "In act to spring."

It is Satyamaya who has filled Pramila's head with nonsense. The Lady Psyche, Mr. Khadilkar has omitted and, as I think, wisely. For Tennyson has not made it clear why that young and charming girl should have been so bitter against male humanity. Lady Blanche "was wedded to a fool", and on that account influenced Princess Ida. Satyamaya was moved by a wish to surpass Parvati who, as one story has it, ran a woman's kingdom in the Himalayas until seduced by Shiv, who made his way into her capital, disguised as a holy and passionless ascetic. In the Darbar the four adventurers have to bear much grotesque abuse of the male sex, of which the following may serve as specimen.

"Men are accursed (mele*) mummers! In their childhood they have faces like women; in their youth the blackguards blacken their faces (i.e., by growing beards) and in their old age, they put a coat of white-wash over the black sins of their youth. In a single life, their faces have three different colours!"

Eventually Pramila, after reading her father's letters, tells the so-called vakil that he may for ten days stay in her kingdom and persuade her if he can to marry Arjuna. It may perhaps here be mentioned that according to Mr. Vaidya, † Arjuna must at this time have been well over 50 and he had already as wives Subhadra, Krishna's sister, and a one-fifth share in Draupadi. But to these ladies, Mr. Khadilkar, exercising a poet's license, makes no reference, and Arjuna appears in his play as an unmarried warrior of about 30. One condition Pramila attaches to the vakil's presence. He and his attendants must in Darbar at any rate speak as if they were women, i.e., must use feminine‡ terminations. To this they have to agree

* The practice of affixing forcible epithets to nouns, which is in English Society usually confined to men, is in Deccan Society usually confined to women. The epithet 'mela,' or 'dead' is a very common abusive word.

† The Mahabharata. A Criticism, p. 145, by Mr. C. V. Vaidya, B. A., LL.B.

‡ This will be best understood by a quotation, "Bayaki Bhasha bolayache mi kabul karite" (instead of Kariton). It is much the same as if a man said in French, "Je suis prête à parler comme une femme."

and the four men's use of them leads to a good deal of merriment. But as the Marathi proverb * has it, "once a beak gets in, a pestle will shortly follow." And now that four men have entered the women's empire, its speedy downfall may confidently be expected. The first women to break their oaths are two lady sepoys, Wagmati and Budhimati. It seems that Arjuna's two old attendants, Maitraya and Jagruka, had been amusing themselves, the former by leering at all the women whom he passed, and Jagruka by fooling old Lady Satyamaya to the top of her bent. At last, bored by her continued lectures, he had set her to search through the Rigveda for types of "Revolting women" which has he said, were to be found there, and he had himself "levanted." Eventually tracked, his evasions to escape punishment reminded Wagmati of her brother's attempts to evade school. Wagmati mentions this to Budhimati who then remembers that her son too must be at school. Following the train of thought thereby started the two women agree to escape from Pramila's clutches by the aid of a Bhil and his wife who have just arrived bringing a message to Rupmaya from her mother, and the two women do eventually get to their homes after a very amusing scene between them and the Bhil's wife who cannot be persuaded that they have not designs on her husband's virtue. The great scene in the play, however, is the wooing of Rupmaya by Pushpadhanwa. With her mother's letter comes to Rupmaya a picture of her betrothed. The sight of it moves her deeply, and

* Chanchu pravesham musul pravesh.

as she is looking at it, Pushpadhanwa, still wearing the disguise of an old man, makes his way to the presence on the pretence of winning her over, if possible to the idea of wedlock with the lover affianced to her in childhood. To her disgust, he at once begins making love to her on his own account and calls her his dear one and himself her slave. Eventually, besides herself with exasperation at the old man's importunity, she confesses her love for Pushpadhanwa. I translate a part of the scene verbatim.

Rupmaya: "O Pushpadhanwa, how would you like to here this old monkey calling the girl whom you love and who loves you, his dear one. Now, you old fool, how do you like that? I refuse to marry Pushpadhanwa only because of the attractions of women's rule. And although you know this you yet pester me. (Pointing to the picture.) Now do you think your old face is more winning than Pushpadhanwa's? Look, accursed one, look at this picture well. To conquer a woman's fancy eyes like these are needed—eyes flashing with light and rounded like a lotus flower in bloom. Open your eyes wide, and looked at this laughing mouth, the haughty beauty of this face, that dear broad breast which bids me embrace it. And then, old cripple, hide your white beard in shame.

Pushpadhanwa: (Disguised) Pretty one, how am I worse than Pushpadhanwa?

Rupmaya: How are you worse? How are you worse?

Pushpadhanwa: (Disguised) My eyes are no less comely than Pushpadhanwa's. I have strength in this my beard to do merely in sport such deeds of valour as Pushpadhanwa had never either in youth or as commander-in-chief accomplished. O dear one, I feel sure that you will throw that picture aside and end by fondling this beard.

Rupmaya : Seeing that I listen to him the old fool begins doting. Accursed one ! Be off with you at once. Get out this instant. If you do not, I'll catch your beard and drag you by it into the courtyard. I'll make such a show of you that you'll remember it all your life. Now out you get.

Pushpadhanwa : (Disguised, kneeling) No, Rupmaya. No. Do what you will but this your slave will linger on at your feet. . . . . . .

Rupmaya : I'll never bring this accursed one to reason until I drag nim out by his beard. [She seizes his beard and pulls. It comes away in her hand. She looks first at the picture and then at Pushpadhanwa and then timidly moving back looks fondly at him. He throws away the rest of his disguise.]

Pushpadhanwa : Rupmaya, I envy the picture in your hand. Pushpadhanwa of the picture has never fallen at your feet. He has never knelt before you or fawned before you. But he can look through my eyes fierce and reddened with the lust of battle* on your lotus cheek to his love's content. And yet on these my (real) eyes, which if denied your love will look at nothing in the world you refuse to smile in fondness. Does this partiality befit you ? I envy the picture. I envy it. And unless I take it from you (he takes it.) Have you

* The picture no doubt represented Pushpadhanwa in armour.

looked at me? Now answer truly. Am I in any way worse to look at than Pushpadhanwa in the picture?

Rupmaya: My lord, what can I say? You disguised yourself as an old man and made me confess my love for you. So what else can this your slave now say to you? But dear one, if any waiting maid were by chance to come here suddenly and were to see you . . . . ?

Pushpadhanwa: Then what will happen? She will tell Pramila that Pushpadhanwa has entered her kingdom. What then?

Rupmaya: Oh, no! I do not want it to be known now. So, do, dear, become an old man as before.

Pushpadhanwa: To gain a woman, men will pretend to be young, old or even women. But I thought that you did not want even to look at that accursed, base, forward, impertinent donkey, at that old fool and cripple.

Rupmaya: O do stop that wretched joke! And do, dear, become again an old man at once . . . "

Eventually by working on her fears Pushpahanwa compels her to promise that she will marry him before re-assuming his disguise. They then flee away together across the border.

Arjuna's suit with Pramila does not proceed so easily. To show the so-called vakil that women are as bold as men, she takes him hunting in the jungle which clothes the banks of the river Saraswati. She wounds a tiger with her arrow. A tigress, its mate, attacks Pramila and her companion. Arjuna snatches from her hands the bow and arrow with which she wishes to defend herself, and with one hand seizing the tigress by the throat and with the other its two paws, holds it at arm's length and then drives it away half-strangled and wholly cowed. This is certainly a tall order. But *tout est permis* to an Aryan hero! Pramila is deeply impressed by this feat, but in order to make her finally yield, Mr. Khadilkar resorts to a device similar to that of Tennyson. It will be remembered that after the Prince's disguise had been betrayed by Cyril's drunken song, Ida in a fury mounted her horse and rode off

> "Hoof by hoof,
> And every hoof a knell to my desires,
> Clanged on the bridge, and then another shriek,
> 'The Head, the Head, the Princess, O the Head!'
> For blind with rage she missed the plank and rolled
> In the river. Out I sprang from glow to gloom.
> There whirled her white robe like a blossomed branch
> Rapt to the horrible fall: a glance I gave,
> No more; but woman vested as I was
> Plunged; and the flood drew; yet I caught her up
> Oaring one arm and bearing in my left
> The weight of all the hopes of half the world
> Strove to buffet to land in vain. A tree
> Was half disrooted from his place and stooped
> To drench his dark locks in the gurgling wave
> Mid-channel. Right on this we drove and caught,
> And grasping down the boughs I gained the shore."

In Mr. Khadilkar's, play, however, Satyamaya or the Lady Blanche gets a ducking also. She has had her fears that in ten days' time the young vakil may make a great deal of love. Partly to watch Pramila and partly to practise austerities, as a good Hindu widow should, she has followed her niece to the banks of the Saraswati. She surprises Pramila and Arjuna in an animated scene, where the latter discloses himself and offers his famous bow "Gandiva" for Pramila to trample on in revenge for his treatment of her bow when the tigress charged. If she does trample on it Arjuna will know that she does not love him. Pramila hesitates and has she does so Satyamaya rushes across a bridge whence she has overheard the discussion in order to trample on it herself. The bridge—no doubt of Hemadpanthi architecture—breaks and Satyamaya is hurled into the river. Arjuna at once springs after her. Primala wishing to share Arjuna's danger refuses to stay behind and the scene closes with the heroic Pandav swimming to shore with a lady on each arm. In Tennyson's play the Princess still remains obdurate and her hero has to fight in the lists, be half-killed by her brother and nursed back to life by herself before she will give way. But Mr. Khadilkar clearly could not so deal with the invincible Arjuna. He therefore makes Satyamaya prove ungrateful. Pramila, shocked by her aunt's ingratitude, confesses her affection for her gallant lover and Satyamaya leaves the story with these words:

"O Adimaya (Parvati) why were not my eyes closed before they saw this sight? I can never teach another woman all my wisdom. Now I go into the forest to perform austerities. Nor shall I ever move from the seat where I shall perform them until the pride of men is conquered and until women's wrists have strength enough to turn men into wet nurses."

In the meantime rumours have reached the capital that the troops with Pramila have become disaffected. The bulk of the women army comes from the capital on the scene in time to face Arjuna's army, who have invaded Pramila's land to see that no harm comes to their general. Pramila, however, intervenes, tells the opposing sides that her reign is over and that she is to be Arjuna's bride and the play closes with the couple's arrival at the King Shvetketu's camp. He blesses the pair, promises to hand them over his lands and wealth before retiring like a true Aryan king to meet death in the practice of austerities, and then turning to his servants, he tells them: "Now all of you go to the capital and arrange for the marriage ceremonies of Arjuna and Pramila."

> "Ask me no more: thy fate and mine are sealed.
> "I strove against the stream and all in vain.
> "Let the great river take me to the main.
> "No more, dear love, for at a touch I yield,
> Ask me no more."

It would, I take it, also be improper to ask what reception Pramila received from Arjuna's family. Was she snubbed by Subhadra? Did Arjuna's one-fifth share of Draupadi ever box her ears? Let us trust not. Hindu women are capable of extraordinary self-sacrifice and submission. Let us rather hope that from the lattice windows of some palace in Hastinapura Pramila smelt the odours and saw the smoke go up from the great Ashwamedha sacrifice which Yudhishthira held when he was finally crowned Emperor of the Universe; that she lived happily until such time at the Pandavas and Draupadi went forth on the Mahaprasthan and that she was still alive when thirty-eight years after the Kurukshetra Yudhishthira took leave of Subhadra with the words "keep in the path of Dharma or Righteousness." So much for Mr. Khadilkar's drama which I have tried to sketch for Anglo-Indian readers. May I venture to hope that in some future play he will throw aside old traditions and use his undoubted talents to picture, without the aid of epic heroes, Indian life as it is? I cannot leave the subject without a word of praise for Mr. Mali, the artist, who has furnished the printed copies* of "A Woman's Revolt." with illustrations. Although the dresses of Arjuna and Pushpadhanwa are Rajput court dresses of to-day and not such as Aryan heroes wore, and although the bridge which broke down at Satyamaya rushed across it has all the appearance of a P. W. D. culvert, these are little matters. The drawing of the figures, especially of the women, is excellent.

* Bayakanche Band, by Mr. K. P. Khadilkar, "Chitrashala Press," Poona.

MAHASHIVRATRA DAY.

To-day the Government officers are closed throughout the Presidency and the weary administrator will have time to seek solace in the latest masterpiece of Victoria Cross or Marie Corelli. Before, however, plunging into its delectable depths, it may not perhaps be without profit or uninteresting to consider why to-day is a holiday. It is the Mahashivratra, the greatest festival of Shiva, the present head of the Hindu triad. The Mahashivratra falls on the 14th day of the dark half of Magh and I have come across two stories told to explain why it does so. They are, of course, mere tales, but religious tales are always of interest and these perhaps especially so far they illustrate the peculiar Hindu doctrine that accidental acts whether of good or evil are as efficacious or as punishable as intentional ones.

The first story is the common one. Once upon a time there lived in Modeshakhya town in Vaidarbha or Berar a wicked king and a worse minister. Both gave full scope to their evil passions, so that in their next life they became respectively a common hunter and a beast of prey. On the 14th Magh Wadya the former was on a hunting expedition when he was suddenly attacked by the latter. To save himself the sportsman climbed a Bel—of all trees the most sacred to Shiva—and as the wild beast strove to clamber after him, he defended himself with one of its branches. In the struggle Bel leaves dropped both from the hunter's hand and the beast's mouth on to where in the sand beneath lay a hidden Shivaite pindi. Now the laying of a Bel leaf on a Shivaite pindi constitutes the offering dearest to Shiva. In an instant the sins of the two were forgiven and Shiva himself appeared in his fiery chariot and bore them away with him to his heaven in Kailasa. In honour of this miracle the 14th Magh Wadya has been deemed to be the holiest of all Shiva's holy days.

The second story is to be found in the Skanda Purâna and was told by the sage Shuk to Shounak and the other Rishis. Once upon a time there lived a king called Mitrasaha of the royal line of Ikshwaku who was learned above all men in the Shastras and the Vedas. His rule extended over the whole earth and its kings everywhere paid him tribute. One day King Mitrasaha while hunting fought with and slew a demon. The demon's brother witnessed the fight and thought how to get vengeance. He feared open battle lest he might meet his brother's fate. So he disguised himself as a cook and obtained employment in King Mitrasaha's household. All went well until the shrâdh anniversary of King Mitrasaha's father. A great feast was prepared and as the demon surpassed in skill all the other cooks, he was entrusted with the preparation of the dinner. Among the guests was the sage Vasishta and in the food prepared for him the demon cook dexterously slipped some human flesh Now Vasishta possessed besides his two eyes an inner eye of knowledge and with it he perceived that he had eaten human flesh. Furious, he cursed King Mitrasaha and condemned him to take the form of a man-eating demon. King Mitrasaha protested that he knew nothing of the matter. Vasishta too learnt through his inner eye of knowledge that King Mitrasaha was not to blame. But the curse of a sage once spoken cannot be recalled. And all that King Mitrasaha could obtain was that the period of his demonhood should be reduced to 12 years. Then compelled by the curse he assumed the guise of a man-eating rakshasa and went into the deep jungle. One day when roaming through the forest he met a Brahman and his wife gathering samidha.* Hungry, he at once seized the Brahman and though the wife vainly begged for his life King Mitrasaha ate him up, picked his bones clean and then went his way. The wife gathered together the bones, made them into a pyre and burnt herself with them. As she burnt she cursed King Mitrasaha and her curse was that on his return to human shape he should die immediately after he had had any intercourse with women. Now King Mitrasaha had heard the wife's speech and on his return to human shape lived a life of perfect chastity and so evaded death. But the guilt of Brahman-hatya or Brahman-killing pursued him and became incarnate as a Chandala woman who always danced before his eyes and

* A samidh (plural, Samidha) is a twig of one of the nine sacred trees with which it is alone permitted to make hom or sacred fire. The nine trees are Palas, Rui, Pimpal, Shami, Khair, Durva, Darbha, Umba and Aghada.

before his eyes alone. Maddened by the sight of this mystic shape he threw aside his kingdom and going into the jungle sought the sage Gautama. Gautama said that there was but one way to obtain release, and that was to go to Gokarna on the 14th Magh Nadya and there worship Shiva. King Mitrasaha asked wherein lay the greatness of Gokarna, and the merit of Magh Wadya Chaturdashi. The sage Gautama replied that on that day in the preceding year he had seen a hideous old Chandala woman lying on the ground and on the point of death when suddenly from heaven came the lord Shiva's fiery chariot. From it his messengers descended and placed in it the Chandalin. "I asked them," said the sage Gautama, "the reason. They replied that the Chandalin was in a former life a Brahman girl called Malini, and possessed beauty that put to shame even Rambha the fairest of the dancing girls of Indra. Her husband died while she was still young and for some days the precepts of her parents and the effects of their early teaching enabled her to triumph over temptations and desires. But her beauty was such that all men longed for her, and at last she yield and so entered upon evil courses. Her parents found out her wickedness and dismissed her from their house. She then became the mistress of a Sudra and gave herself up unrestrainedly to the eating of meat and the drinking of wine. One day when she could obtain no meat she killed a young heifer and eating half of it escaped the neighbour's blame by crying out that a panther had killed it. She died not long afterwards and when her soul came to Yama's Court, Chitragupta's* record showed that she had committed *gohatya*, and she was at once consigned to the blackest Hell. In her next life, she became a blind, leprous and filthy Chandala woman whom not even a Chandala would marry. To-day she was begging from the pilgrims to Gokarna, but all refused her alms. At last, one pilgrim in derision placed a Bel leaf in her hand. In anger she threw it away and it fell on a hidden Shivaite pindi. Then the lord of Kailas' heart melted in pity for her, and he sent his chariot and his messengers to bear her away to his heaven. With these words the messengers and the chariot bore away the Chandala woman to the snowy mountain tops of Kailas." Hearing the words of the sage Gautama, hope once more came to the heart of King Mitrasaha, and he made his way to Gokarna, and on the 14th day of the Krishna or dark-half of Magh he fasted and each watch of the night he worshipped Shiva by placing on his holy pindi the leaves of the Bel tree. And the following day he fed Brahmans and gave gifts to the poor and the blind, and in this wise he too obtained the mercy of the lord Shiva. The image of the Chandala woman faded from King Mitrasaha's eyes and he knew that he was freed from the most terrible of all sins that a man may commit—the sin of Brahman-hatya or Brahman murder.

* Chitragupta is the recording angel.

PROVERBIAL PHILOSOPHY IN WESTERN INDIA.

I.—THE SAYINGS OF KATHIAWAR.

The day has in England long gone by when the wise saws and well-worn sayings of some time honoured member of she family carried weight in a discussion. If one practised in ordinary conversation the art of introducing happily rhyming proverbs, one would soon have no one left with whom to converse and beyond that of an intolerable bore one would have achieved no other reputation. Yet two hundred years ago, things were different. The Squire Westerns whom Macaulay in the famous third chapter of his history describes as ruling with an iron rod their feudal domains, yet standing awestruck in the London Streets at the sight of the Lord Mayor's show, used the old English proverbs as the staple buttress of their arguments. One can imagine what a formidable engine of oppression proverbs, such as

> A woman, a spaniel and a walnut tree
> The more you beat them the better they be;

and "Spare the rod, spoil the child" must have been when it was considered almost impious to question the superior wisdom of one's forefathers. Indeed, I seem to have an unpleasant recollection in my own childhood of what then at any rate appeared to me to be a misuse of the latter aphorism. But the saws of Squire Western and the simples of his helpmeet have gone their way, and an English proverb now is hardly ever used, save to distort it into a paradox.

Western India, however, has not yet reached the paradox stage of human development. And I have myself seen a happily applied proverb close more than once an intricate discussion, and an Indian proverb on a European's lips invariably fills a native audience with an immense and often excessive respect for his acquaintance with their language. Hereafter I may deal with the proverbs common amongst the Marathas. But in this chapter I shall confine myself to the Gujarati sayings of Kathiawar, which yields to no country in its appreciation of proverbial wisdom. I do not intend—far from it—to give an exhaustive list, but it may be of some interest to my readers to know which of the several hundred proverbs, which may be found in published collections are in ordinary conversation most commonly used.

Sometimes, although rarely, Gujarati proverbs seem almost translations of the English equivalent such as "parej ej uttam osad" (dieting is the best medicine), which is nearly a reproduction of "Diet cures more than the doctors." So also "dukhnu osad dahada" (the cure for grief is days)—"Time is the best healer." But more often the different conditions of like necessitate a different clothing for the same idea. We say "all that glitters is not gold." The Kathiwadi peasant says "all that is white is not milk" (dholu etalu dudh nahi). We say "a full purse never lacks friends." He says "on a green tree there are many parrots" (lila wanna suda ghana). We say "penny wise and pound foolish"; he says "it is useless to plug up the sink pipe and leave the door open" ("khale ducha ne darwajo moklo"). Is there not an Irish story which points out the uselessness of padlocking the gate when there are gaps in the hedge? However to match "a bribe in the lap blinds the eyes," he also makes a reference to money. "The sight of gold makes a saint wobble" (sonu dekhi muni chale).

We who are an animal-loving nation make a considerable use of the domestic ones in our sayings. We say "Don't count your chickens before they are hatched." The Kathiawadis say elliptically "Wheat in the field and the child in the womb" (ghau khetman ne beta petman). We say "Let sleeping dogs lie." They say "Do not rouse the sleeping snake" (sutelo sap jagadvo nahi). We say "We all think our own geese swans." They say "Chagan Magan's children are of gold, while every one else's are of dung." (Chagan magan to sona na ne parka chokra garana). We say "A crying crow bears bad news." They say "A weeping man means a death" (rose jay te muvano samachar lave). On the other hand, animals are not wholly absent from the Kathiawadi's proverbs. They say "To make an elephant out of an atom" (rajnu gaj karavun) instead of "A mountain out of a mole hill," and they have elaborated "Barking dogs do not bite," into "Barking dogs do not bite nor do thundering clouds rain" (bhasya kutta kate nahin ne gajya megh varse nahin).

Some of the best Kathiawadi proverbs employ similes from the village trades. The proverb "A carpenter thinks of nothing but babulwood" (sutar-nu man bovaliaman) may be translated "There is nothing like leather." On the other hand, we have no proverbial equivalent for "An idle barber shaves the footstools" (navro) hajam patala munde), and must fall back on that terror of boyhood, Dr. Watts, for "Satan finds some mischief still for idle hands to do." Nevertheless excessive energy meets with approval in "puchhtan puchhtan lanka javey" (by asking and asking one can get to Ceylon). That the village savkar is sometimes outwitted is proved by "Sehth kem tanano to ke labhe lobhe" ("How did the sheth come to grief? He was too clever by half.") The brief reign of the village cartman while he drives his cart finds expression in "we must sing the songs of the man in whose cart we sit (jene vele bessie tena git gaie). It may be translated "who pays for the fiddler may call the tune." But the village tailor, who is mentioned by implication in "Cut your coat according to your cloth" receives no recognition in "make your grass bed according to the size of your body" (sod pramane satharo).

As might have been expected, the common round of household duties provides proverbs in Gujarati as well as in English, although they are not necessarily similar in the two languages. "A stitch in time saves nine' finds an equivalent in "Early plantains are really plantains" (velae male te kela). "It never rains but it pours" may be translated in two ways :—"When it rains it rains in the hedges" (varse to vadma varse) or—and the second proverb gives the sense more accurately—"She went to look for her son and she lost her husband" (!ene geie put or khoe aie khasam). The poor lady certainly deserved sympathy. So, too, did "the good wife who went to her father-in-law and got scolded by the unfaithful wife" (dahi sasare jay ane gandi shikhaman de)! A proverb very typical of Indian home life is the following "chas man makan jay ane rand fuvad kehevay" (when butter goes with the buttermilk the wife gets called a slut). The explanation is to be found in the Gujarati custom of distributing the butter-milk from which a large quantity of butter has been churned. The careful housewife is expected to see that her friends get none of the butter! Another proverb which also inculcates, although sarcastically, the lesson that charity should begin at home is "gharma chokra ghanti chate ne apudhyane ato" (the children of the house lick the grinding mill while the spiritual teacher gets the flour). Had this saying been brought to the notice of the "Shepherd" in Pickwick he might have avoided serious trouble at the hands of Mr. Weller. "The child is father of the man" finds a mate in "the qualities of a son may be seen from his cradle" (putrana lakshan palnamathi janay). The French fable of 'Le pot de fer et le pot de terre' may be pitted against "If the short man goes with the tall one, he may not die, but he will get very sick" (lamba jode tuko jay mare nahi pan mando thay). "A short life and a merry one" is rather neatly translated by "four days of moonlight" (char divasnu chandarnu), which in turn recalls Moore's refrain.

"The best of all ways to lengthen your days, is to take a few hours from the night, my dear." "A little pot is soon hot" is on the other hand more felicitous than "the weak man has a bad temper" (kamzor ne gusso bot); and "What the eye does not see the heart does not grieve" than "not to see is not to mourn" (dekhvun nahi ne dajeun nahin). Yet we have nothing so good as "to a wooden god give a slipper" as an offering (lakdana devne khasdani puja).

Some of the Kathiawadi proverbs have, like some English ones, a deeper meaning than appears on the surface. "From afar the mountains are beautiful" (Dungaro durthi raliamuna) corresponds with "Distance lends enchantment to the view." So also "As the father, so are the sons, and as the banian tree, so are the branches" (Bap teva beta and wad teva teta) is a close match for "As the twig is bent so the tree is inclined." "Hope deferred maketh the heart sick" finds an equivalent in "the hope that rests on others is continual despair" (parki ash saday nirash). My official readers will probably after this wonder why that pest, the youthful candidate for office, bothers them so frequently. An answer will, I think, be found in "Ap mua pacchi dub gaie udnia" (when I have died the world is drowned) a proverb which like Louis XV's "Après moi le déluge" must have emanated from an extremely self-centred person.

I would, however, suggest an unfailing method to all those who are at a loss how to get rid of a wholly unqualified, but pertinacious claimant. Ask him quietly if he has ever heard the story of the

"Bavo and the soni." The tale runs that a certain Bavo or religious mendicant went to a goldsmith's shop and asked to be given a lump of gold. The soni began at length and with many interpolations of "My dear young friend" to explain that gold was a valuable thing and not to be given away in lumps. At last the Bavo got sick to death of the lecture and said "I knew all that, and I did not fancy you would give it to me, but I thought that there was no harm in asking." As a reply to the question the candidate invariably grins feebly and makes for the door. Should a last spark of hope induce him to linger on the threshold and to enumerate his imaginary merits, then fire him out with the proverb "Praised Khijdi sticks to the teeth" (vakhanani Khijdi dante valge) and the disappointed one will, like Slipper in the adventures of an Irish R. M., "vanish like a dream."

II.—SAYINGS OF THE DECCAN.

In the first chapter of this series I ventured to discuss some of the more common Kathiawadi proverbs. I would now place before my readers some of the wise sayings of the Deccan and they will probably be struck at the absence of that resemblance which they might have expected from the common origin of the two languages—Marathi and Guzarathi.

A country so long under orthodox priestly rule as the uplands of the Sahyadris not unnaturally possesses several proverbs dealing with religion or with its ministers. The most delightful one to my mind is "Laksh pradakshina ani ek paisa dakshina." It means literally "the going round the idol 100,000 times and at the end a gift of one pice as an offering to the Brahmans.' We are ourselves not unacquainted with the type of religious enthusiast who may be summed up in Mr. Lewis Carroll's description of the Snark:

> "At charity meetings he stands at the door
> And collects though he does not subscribe."

"Melya vanchun swarga disat nahin" (one cannot reach heaven without dying) expresses an idea similar to that in "Il faut souffrir pour être beau" and we will probably all agree with the excellent maxim "jar man asel changla tar kathavatint Ganga" (if your mind is pure, it is as a good as having Ganges water in your platter). A very common proverb too of this class is "bazarant turi bhat bhatnila mari" (the Brahman beat his wife because of the turi (pulse) in the bazaar). The tale runs that a Brahman priest who had by means foul or fair secured a little money wished to give himself a good dinner and directed his wife to buy him some pulse in the bazaar. The question arose as to how the pulse should, when bought, be cooked, and an acrimonious discussion terminated with the whacking of the unruly housewife. The proverb is ordinarily used in the same sense as 'Don't count your chickens before they are hatched.'

The animal kingdom, especially the donkey, finds a considerable place in Marathi aphorisms. "Apale garje gadhava raje" (in our need we call an ass a king) may be rendered by 'necessity makes strange bedfellows' "Ghadhavaya pudhen wachali gita kalcha gondhal bara hota" (if you read the Gita before an ass, he will think that yesterday's kick up was better fun). Well perhaps the ass was not quite so wrong, for have we not De La Rochefoucauld's authority for 'Qui vit sans folie n'est pas si sage qu'il croit'? Another proverb meaning also 'Don't cast pearls before swine' is "Gadhawas gulachi chav kay" (an ass will have no relish for joggery). And the poor beast's proper occupation is laid down in "Jyacha tyala ani gadhva ojhayala" (the only use of an ass is to carry burdens). I have only discovered one saying which mentions the horse and that is the phrase "ghodya evadi chuk" (a mistake as big as a horse). The mistake must have been a real "howler" and probably occurred in some youthful subaltern's exercise for the Lower Standard Hindustani! But there used to be a saying commonly used by grooms to their horses when they refused to drink "Dhanaji wa Santaji panya madhayen tula distat kay" (do you see Dhanaji and Santaji in the water). This saying had a great historical interest for it dated from the time when Dhanaji Jadav and Santaji Ghorpade were the terror of the Grand Army of Aurangzeb. The cow finds a place two or three times. "Gaine gay phalat nahin' implies that one poor wretch cannot help another. Our vulgar saying 'It's the poor as helps the poor' expresses a different point of view. "Salyachi gay ani malyache vasru" (the weaver's cow and the mali's calf) implies that a clean sweep has been made of everything. Lastly, "Odhal gurun ani oshal bayako" means 'a straying cow is like a shameless wife.' No doubt both suffer from the *kakoethes vagandi.* The buffalo is honoured by the delightful maxim "Melia mhashila panch sher dudh" (the dead buffalo always gave five seers of milk.) It reminds one of the story of the lady who when asked whether she had ever heard of any one who was absolute perfection, replied 'O constantly! she was my husband's first wife.' The jackal, the dog, the camel, the kid, the cat, the crocodile and the ant are honoured by a proverb a piece—"Kolha kakadila raji (a jackal is satisfied with a cucumber) may be rendered Hunger is the best sauce.' "Andhala dalato aani kutra pit khato" (the blind man grinds and the dog eats the flour). This saying is generally used of a man whose brains have been sucked. "Untawaril shahana" (he who is on a camel is a wise man) has a story connected with it. A buffalo got its head into an earthen vessel and could not extricate it without breaking the jar which he did not wish to do. All his friends gave him advice, but a man riding on a camel suggesting cutting off the buffalo's head and thereby saving the vessel. The phrase is used of a foolish busy body: "Jogyache karde ladke" (a yogi's kid is like a daughter to him). So also we use the Biblical phrase 'one ewe lamb.' "Manjaras undir saksh"—a mouse as witness for a cat—implies that a servant must give evidence as his master pleases and that therefore his testimony is worthless. The crocodile is to be found in "Susanbai tujhi pat phar mau" (O lady crocodile, your back is very soft.) The idea is that by thus flattering the crocodile she may be induced safely to carry you across the river in which she lies. Safely on the other side you send her about her business with a good kick in the stomach. Lastly, the elephant and the ant find a place in " mungi houn sakhar khavi ; pan hatti houn lakde khaun nayet " (It is all very well for an ant to eat sugar, but an elephant should not live on sticks) ; in other words, one must live according to one's station. This idea finds more comic expressions in " nesen tar shalu nesen, nahitar nagvi basen " (If I wear clothes I shall put cloth of gold, if not I shall sit with 'nodings on'). The gender shews that the speaker was a lady.

The time-honoured maxim 'Spare the rod and spoil the child' finds an equivalent in—" Chhadi lage chhum chhum vidya yei ghum ghum "—which we may translate in the following couplet :

" The more the urchins feel the whacks
The more their little brains they'll tax."

The following three proverbs have their humorous side : " Doi dharala tar bodaka, hati dharala tar rodaka " (If you try to catch him by the head you will find that he has shaved it ; if you catch his hand it will be so thin as to slip through your fingers). The person alluded to must have been as elusive as Mr. Balfour, when many years ago the late Sir William Harcourt described him as 'slipppery as an eel.' " Jyachi lage chad to ude tad mad (he who is sought after holds himself as high as a toddy palm or a cocoanut tree) describes the condition known in America as a badly swollen head. Lastly, " gajrachi pungi wajli tar wajli nahitar khaun takli (if you " can play a tune on a carrot well and good, if you fail you can always eat it) expresses the same idea as the well known Irish saying "Be aisy, and if you can't be aisy, be as aisy as you can." I must however confess that an attempt to play a tune on this vegetable would almost be as good an illustration of nonsense as that of the youthful essayist 'it would be nonsense, Sir, to bolt a door with a boiled carrot.'

Two somewhat sad proverbs are "Daiv detopan, karm nete (the gods give, but karma takes away) and "Dushkalacha terava mahina" (a famine year) has always thirteen months). The first because it expresses the terrible idea that no matter how we strive we cannot escape the punishment of sins committed in a former existence. And the second because it alludes to the endless waiting until the next year's monsoon comes to relieve the kunbi's suffering.

Here are two sayings which must respectively have been invented by a pessimist and an optimist. The first is "Udima karitan sola bara sheta karitan doivar bhara" (If you trade you will get 12 annas for every 16 (spent) and if you till you will have to carry loads on your head). The second runs "God karun khaven mau karun nijaven (If it is not sweet make it so and if your bed is not soft make it so). Then come two which must have emanated from a cynic "Labha pekshan bholyachi asha." The fool's hopes exceed (possible) gain" and bara koshavar paus, shivecha raut, panivathyachi ghagar. (There are 3 things very difficult to get, the rain falling 24 miles away, the village headman and the jar you left at the watering place.)

Here is a proverb which shows how well beggars fare in kindly India "Bhikeshwar kinva Lankeshwar." "It is best to be the king of the beggars and next best to be king of Lanka," *i.e.*, Eldorado, for when Ravan ruled there the bricks were all of gold. Then there are two which inculcate homely prudence "Bail gela ni zhopa kela" (He built a shed after his ox had gone *i.e.*, do not lock the stable after the horse has bolted.) "Pudhchyas thech magcha shahana (The one behind may profit by the tripping of the man in front).

Here is one very amusing one—

Panya madhyen masa
Zhop gheto kasa
Javen tyachya vansha
Tewhan kale

I have translated it as follows :—

Let him who'd learn how 'tis that sleep
Cometh to little fishes
Become a fish and swim the deep
He'll learn then when he wishes.

I have in vain sought for proverbs in which the English are the subject of adverse comment, and this might be taken to heart by those who believe that Poona is full of sedition and seditious people. But, I believe, that sometimes in the streets one may hear little girls sing the following nursery rhyme that dates from the days of the conquest :—

Hattichya sonde vari
Theveli menbutti
Sarya Punyachi keli matti
Ingrejani, Ingrejani !

It has little or no meaning, for what connection there is between the elephant and the English, takes some thinking out. However, such as it is, I translate it as follows :—

> Upon the elephant's trunk now sways
> the lamp—and O ! the pity,
> The English and the English ways
> Have ruined Poona City !

III.—THE SAYINGS OF THE PARSEES.

It is usually supposed that the language of the Parsees is ordinary Gujarati, and, no doubt, in recent years, there have been great and successful efforts on behalf of Parsees with literary tastes to equal the purity of style attained by the Gujarati-speaking Hindus. But the great bulk of the Parsee community speak a dialect which has marked peculiarities and varies as much from the Gujarati of Kathiavad as Milanese does from Tuscan. And to this dialect the older members adhere with a certain pride and resent the use of what they call "bania's lingo." As an instance of this, I may mention, that a leading Parsee barrister whose children had been educated at Rajkot, told me that when his son visited his aunt she said with some asperity "are tune sun thayun; tu wania jevo bolech." (What on earth has happened to you, you are talking like a bania !) In this Parsee dialect have grown up a number of proverbs, many of which would be quite unintelligible to a Hindu. In the course of this paper I propose to deal with the sayings of this strange community who for many centuries have lived together with, yet apart from, their Hindu neighbours. I will not guarantee that all the ensuing aphorisms are peculiar to the Parsees, although many of them are. But all of them are commonly used by Parsees even if some are not unknown to the Hindus also.

The most remarkable trait in these Parsee proverbs is the bitterness with which the rival towns —Bombay, Bulsar, Cambay, Surat, Navsari and Broach—speak of each other. This enmity between commercial cities is not, however, unknown in Europe. Here is a proverb that must be extremely galling to Surati pride, 'kiun Surati ? to bi murvat ki murti' (What ! a Surati ! then (you see) the image of a shameless man). It is the ladies, however, who come in for the severest abuse. The next two proverbs are really delightful. The first is said by a Bombay lady of a Broach woman.

> "Bharuchi Bhaji chapre chapre nachi,
> So chhana baera pan khichri to kachi ne kachi."

(the Broach woman jumped from roof, and to roof, although a hundred cow-dung cakes were burnt yet the khichri remained uncooked). In other words, she was a wanton slut. The sting of the gibe is in the words "baera" and "kachi ne kachi." which are Broach colloquialisms. The Broach woman, however, rose to the occasion and retorted "Mumbaini modan gharni Dhoban" (The great lady from Bombay is the washer-woman of every house). This is a hit at the Europeanised Parsee ladies who go out to tea-parties and then, so it is implied in the proverb, talk scandal. The word "dhoban" has much the same sense as our expression, "to wash one's dirty linen in public." The Surat lady is again the victim in the following:

("Suratni nari evi sari ke khun karine kutwa chali)" (The Surat woman is so good that she will commit murder and then at the ensuing funeral be the loudest mourner present!). The weak points of the Cambay, Broach, Surat and Navsari ladies find expression in the following:—

Khambatan khodiyan ne Bharuchi chadiyan
Suratan fankri ne Nosakri Aakri.

(The Cambay woman is ill-made, the Broach woman is a tell-tale, the Surat woman is a flirt and the Navsari woman is hot tempered). I am told that the only reason why Navsari was left off so lightly was because it is the home of the priests of whom the couplet-maker, perhaps, stood in awe. However, if the rival townsmen said hard things of each others' ladies they were quite ready to lavish praise on themselves. The following proverb was written by a Bulsar man of Bulsar:—

Wadun gam te Valsad saghla gamnu taran
"Parsioman Kahanji ne Vanioman Naran."

(Bulsar is the mighty city, the salvation of all other cities. Among the Parsees we have our Kahanji, and among the Banias we have our Naran.) This reminds one of the old Athenian saying that a Corinthian could never travel without for ever talking of "Dios Korinthos" (glorious Corinth). And did not Bernier, who saw Delhi in its heydey, contrast it unfavourably with the splendours of Paris as seen from the Pont Neuf!

A number of Parsee proverbs deal with the never-dying feud between the mother-in-law and the daughter-in-law. For the 'belle-mère' of Parsee tradition is, as she is among Hindu families, not the wife's but the husband's mother. Here is a delightful one.

> Dinio bandhyun dahi
> Jiluo tano chhas
> Gulio tavyun ghi
> No Sasuji jamo khas.

Dini prepared the curds, Jilu the butter-milk, Guli cooked the ghee, and then the mother-in-law had a rare good meal).

A similar hit at the mother-in-law's gluttony is to be found in the following :—

> "Juar dali sher no git gaya ter
> Sasue muki rotli to ankho aya pher."

(She (the daughter-in-law) ground a seer of jowari and while doing so sang thirteen songs. (But) the mother-in-law gave her only one chapatti and she (the daughter-in-law) felt quite giddy with hunger). The poor thing !

The point of the thirteen songs may puzzle some of my readers. It lies in the fact that all Indian women sing while grinding grain, and this finds expression in the Marathi proverb "jatyavar baslyas git athavte" (one remembers songs while sitting at the grinding mill). The point of the passage is that the poor daughter-in-law sat so long grinding that she was able to sing thirteen songs from beginning to end !

Yet another saying against the mother-in-law is to be found in.

> 'Mari Sasu evi bholi
> Ke nahi dekhado diwali ke holi.

(My mother-in-law is so good that she will not show me either diwali or holi). It is scarcely necessary to remark that the work good is meant "sarcastic." But in fairness to the mother-in-law, it should be added, that an old-fashioned Hindu Holi festival is not the best place for a young married woman!

Another rather amusing saying is "Sasus bhange te kahaleda ne wahu bhange te thikra" (Whenever the mother-in-law breaks anything it is only "Kahelada," but whenever the wife breaks anything it is a "thikra") "Kahaleda" and "thikra" are earthen pots of which the "thikra" is the more expensive. The meaning is that the mother-in-law minimises her own faults and exaggerates her daughter-in-law's and to use Butler's words:

> "Compounds for sins she is inclined to
> By damning those she has no mind to."

After all these nasty remarks at the mother-in-law's expense, it is not surprising to be told that when a mother-in-law dies then the daughter-in-law attains happiness, (sasu giyi savarat ne vahune avi navarat.)

There are some proverbs, however, which take the side of the step-mother and the mother-in-law. Here are one or two. "Sat sok jaje pan be savka por na jati" (Be if you like) the seventh wife of your husband, but do not enter a house where there are even two step-children!) "Sasu khadhi sasaro khadho, khadho gherjamai ne bar gamna gadheda khadha, to be nahin dharai" (She (the wife) ate up (talked to death), her mother-in-law, her father-in-law, her son-in-law and all the donkeys of twelve villages and she is not yet satisfied—i. e. goes on talking—). We might compare the English saying sometimes used of an old woman. "She would talk the hindleg off a donkey." Then again "satwa seta ne barni patli, vahune chatar palang ne sasune khatli." The first line is meaningless and like the "Dingdong Dell" "Hickery Dickery-Dock" of our nursery rhyme is simply introduced for jingle. The last line is expressive, "The wife has a European bedstead with mosquito curtains, while the mother-in-law has a little native cot." The mother-in-law like the lady of the Rhine, felt no doubt the 'spretae injuria formae.'

The mother-in-law is not the only victim. Here is one that must excite avuncular disgust. "Kaka mama kekevana ne ganthe hoi te levana" (you must call them kaka (paternal uncle) and mama (maternal uncle) but they will rob you of everything you have). The word "gantha" is the knot at the end of the scarf in which natives usually carry their money. The paternal grandmother is chastised in the following:—"Mamai ankhman samai, bapai chulie kapai." (The mother's mother is the apple of my eye, but I could cut up father's mother with a mutton chopper).

If we leave the subject of relatives we find a number of other amusing proverbs. "Latko matko ne soparino larko" (full of flirting and coquetry and worth a bit of betelnut). The lady to whom this was applied must have resembled the heroine of Burns' original version of "coming through the rye."

Some sayings illustrate certain national peculiarities. It is said that some Parsees are in the habit of saying "Shu, shu" "what, what" just as in English one hears "what ?" frequently added without cause to the end of a sentence. The retort to such a misuse of language is crushing.

> 'Shu, shuna bacha ne lasanni kali,
> Tari Sasu gadhere chadi."

(What, whats' children and a piece of garlic, your mother-in-law rode on an ass.) The point of this polite observation is that in Musalman times unchaste women were made to ride with inked features on a donkey and face tailwards. One might compare with this, the French saying used to little boys when they say "Quoi ?" instead of the politer "comment ?" "Quoi, quoi, les corbeaux sont dans les bois."

The custom indicated in the following proverb is that of old-fashioned Parsees who, invariably when asked after their health, reply that they are feeling rather poorly, just as an English peasant will always say that he has the "rheumatiz."

> "Sasu kanse, vahu karanje ne pal palina petman dukhe,
> ne varo to jetlo ne tetlo uthe."

(The mother-in-law groans, the wife moans, the maid servant has a pain in her stomach but the amount of food consumed never varies).

Personal peculiarities are the subject of some proverbial comment. "Baro bohetar lakhanvalo" (the squint-eyed man has 72 tricks) and "thuthani rand ne thamko bhari" (a cripples' mistress walks with great airs and graces). The blind-man and the one-eyed share the following proverb. "Andhlo hikmati ane kano kepheyati" (A blind man is full of tricks and a one-eyed man full of dodges). This idea of the wiliness of the one-eyed man seems universal in India. Colonel Tod mentions the belief as strongly rooted in Rajasthan, and it finds expression in the following Kathiawadi proverb :—

Kanio nar kok sadhu
Talio nar kok nirdhan
Khokhad danta kuk murkha
Danta kok mijhra

(A one-eyed is rarely a saint, a bald man is rarely poor, a man with projecting teeth is rarely a fool and a man with grey eyes is rarely generous).

I tried hard, but in vain, to discover the grounds why these particular qualities were associated with these peculiarities. As a matter of fact, this arbitrary association is not entirely confined to the East. I have seen used by M. Armand Silvestre the phrase "Il riait comme un bossu" *i. e.*, he was laughing outrageously. And yet it is difficult to understand why the mirth of a hump-backed man should be so wholly unrestrained.

SAYINGS OF THE MUSULMANS.

I have now come to the last of this series—the proverbial sayings of the Musulmans. It is no doubt true that in no part of the Western Presidency is Musulmani the spoken language of the bulk of the people. Nevertheless there live, scattered from Cutch to Kanara, countless Mahomedan families who talk amongst themselves some or other dialect of Hindustani, and here and there may be found aristocratic groups whose Urdu may well compete with that of Delhi or Lucknow. Hindustani, moreover, from its former place in the mouths of Northern rulers has acquired a peculiar position as the medium between the master and the servant. A well-known Parsi pleader mentioned to me that his father preferred to talk Hindustani to his Ahmedabadi servants, although, the mother tongue of master and man was Gujarati. He found that they better obeyed his orders when delivered in the former tongue. Hindustani has similarly descended as an appendage of Baber's empire to the English rulers. English ladies use no other tongue in Indian households. Every day in Bombay carriages are ordered in a strange jargon, which, if not Hindustani, is certainly nothing else. Thus, if for no other reason, Hindustani may claim a place among Western Indian tongues, as the language of the Mogal and the memsahib of the "fortiter in modo" and the "fortissime in re."

I must, however, forestall criticism by admitting that in many of the proverbs which follow the grammar and the wording are not that of Delhi. I have collected Musulmani sayings as I have heard them, and if I were to alter their phrasing they would no longer belong properly to Western India. On the other hand, some of the provebs are almost pure Persian and should satisfy the highest of high proficiency scholars.

I shall begin with a very pretty aphorism which expresses in poetical form the common French saying "les grands hommes les grands soucis les petits hommes les petits soucis."

Burre burre ko dukh hai
Chote se dukh dur
Tare sab nyare rahe
Grahe chandra aur sur

I have translated it as follows :—

> He knows not happy, humble one
> What great men's sorrows are.
> Eclipses darken moon and sun
> And spare the lowly star.

But most of the Musulmani proverbs which I have met contain merely plain household truths. "Nach na jane angan terha" [(the dancing girl) who cannot dance (complains that) the courtyard is crooked] may be translated "a bad workman quarrels with his tools." "Our proverb "speech is silvern, silence is gold" finds expression in two Hindustani sayings 'sabse barri chup' (silence is the greatest of all things.) "Ek chup aur hazar sukh" (one silence and a thousand comforts). And it may possibly be in unconscious recognition of the advantages of silence that the indignant Englishman is for ever saying to his Aryan brother "Chup raho!" "Where there's a will there's a way" finds a neat equivalent in "marzi ho to sab kuchh hai." "If there is a will then there is everything," and "ittifak kuwvat hai" is a literal rendering of 'union is strength.' "Awwal sonch pechi bol"— "Listen first and speak afterwards" contains no doubt sound advice. But in opposition to it may be quoted the Gujarati saying "lat pacchi wat"— "kick him first and take his explanation afterwards," and the latter will probably commend itself to the "strong officer!" "Kathki handia ekhi dafa charhti hai—" "a wooden pot can only be placed on the fire once," is a rather subtle way of saying that an impostor is soon found out, and that honesty is the best policy.

An amusing equivalent for "do not count your chickens before they are hatched" is to be found in "sut na kapas kolhuse lath tham latha" (he quarrelled with his spinning wheel before he had bought either cotton or yarn), naturally the result was disaster. A delightfully elliptical phrase is the following: "In tilon men tel nahin" (In those sesamum seeds there is no oil)." It is used when a beggar tries in vain to get money from a miser and learns too late that it is useless to try to tap that Pactolus! Another reference to a miser is found in the following, "damri ki barhai taka sir mundai" "he defended himself from the charge of not providing a barber for his mother by saying why should I pay a taka" (1 pice) for shaving the head of an old woman who is only worth a 'damri' (half a pie)!" The mother-in-law does not receive in Hindustani proverbs—the wholesale abuse showered on her by the Parsees and Gujaratis. But the following saying, frequently used to the young wife, when she quarrels with her husband's mother hardly gives a flattering idea of her nature. "Darya men rahna aur magar machch se byr" (To live in the sea and to have enmity with the magar machch). It is impossible accurately to translate "magar machch" for it is applied indiscriminately to any dangerous aquatic or amphibious animal. And if one complains to an Indian of the bewildering looseness of such an expression he will sooner or later give one politely to understand that for his part it is a matter of indifference whether any particular beast is a shark, a whale, an alligator or a hippopotamus.

"Dudh ka jala chach phunk phunk kar pita hai" (He who has been scalded by milk blows repeatedly on buttermilk before he will drink it) is the Hindustani rendering of the Kathiavadi proverb "sapno karadyo dhori thi bhie." (He who has been bitten by a snake is afraid of a piece of rope). Both may be translated as "A burnt child dreads the fire." It is, however, difficult to give a concise rendering of "Mitha hap hap karwa thu thu." It means that things when sweet were gobbled up but when bitter spat out. The saying is as a rule used to a servant who did not grumble until things went badly, or of a friend who deserted one when trouble came. Perhaps the nearest English equivalent would be "rats leave a sinking ship."

From among so many household proverbs the household animals are not omitted. "Billi ki khwab men chichre." (In the cat's dreams figure mutton scraps). By day, however, the cat seems to be over-sensitive to ridicule "Khisayni billi khamba noche" (a cat that has been laughed at scratches the door-post). The dog finds a place in the two following proverbs "choti kutti jalebiyan ki rakhwali" (it is no use appointing the little dog as a guard over the sweetmeats); and "aamri ki handia gaikutte ki zat pahchhan" (only a worthless pot was lost and the dog's nature was recognised). The latter saying is employed when some servant's fraud has been detected at little cost and the master is "well rid of a rogue."

Nor is the snake, the household enemy, overlooked: "sarp nikal gaya lakir pita karo." (The snake has gone, so why puzzle your head about its trail). This proverb has somewhat the same meaning as "it is no use shutting the stable door after the horse has been stolen"; and the derivative expression "lakir ka fakir" a man who following the trail rather than the snake is applied to a blind devotee of ancient rather than modern learning. The carrion kite, may, in India, almost be called a household animal and there is no questioning the truth of the following "chil ke ghonsle men mas kahan" (you will not find meat in a carrion kite's nest). Lastly, the elephant is the hero of a somewhat striking aphorism "Hathi ke dant dikhane ke aur hain, khane ke aur hain" (an elephant has one set of teeth for show and another for use). This saying is curiously enough used of a hypocrite and recalls the biting jest that was made of the shifty and treacherous Duke of Anjou. He was the French Henry III's brother and small-pox had left him with two tips to his nose. But as an enemy observed "Un prince qui avait deux faces devrait bien avoir deux nez."

Some other Hindustani proverbs are merely amusing while some indicate the national characteristics of the Indian Musulman. Among the former are "khud andha aur aftab siyah" (blind himself he calls the sun black); "nange se khuda khof rakhta hai" (God even is afraid of the shameless man); "Tum ham razi, to kya kare kotwal aur kazi" (If you and I agree, what harm can the kotwal and the kazi do us?). In other words, it is better to keep out of chancery. "Bare bhai so bare bhai, chote bhai so subhan Allah" is a phrase not infrequently applied to brothers born in the purple. It may be translated—The elder brother—well, what *can* you expect of an elder brother?

and the younger brother, well, God be praised! Arcades ambo, *id est*, blackguards both! Among the second class are "jaldi ka kam shaitan ka." (To do work quickly is of the devil). Undue haste is hateful to the slow and rather pompous Islamite, whose love of vain show is indicated in the two following sayings. "Makan men ata nahin aur amma puriya pakati hai" (There is no flour in the house but mamma pretends she is making cakes); "Das ghar mangna lekin masalchi rakhna" (To beg at ten houses and yet keep a servant).

One more saying and I have done. I write it with some reluctance, nevertheless I trust that my Poona readers will accept my assurance that it is not with any intention of hurting their feelings that I quote a couplet which after all hits my own countrymen as hard as it hits them I only mention it because of its historical interest, for it must clearly have been invented sometime when the English and the Marathas were still contending for the sovereignty of India.

"Angrez ki siyahi se Hindki gadai bihtar
Dakhani shahi se sau bar kasai bihtar."

"Better to be a beggar wandering all over India than be pestered with English ink. Better a hundred times be a butcher than feel the rule of the Deccani."

As one reads one wonders from whom the saying first came. Was it some Rohilla Afghan who thought of the great and merciless Alla-ud-din, the Indian Sikandar, who conquered Gujarat and utterly sacked Chitor? Or was it some Mogal noble who recalled the lion stock of Zingis and

Timur—the knightly Humayun to whom the Udaipur Queen sent her bracelet, Jehangir, the toper king, who loved the beautiful Nur Mahal, Shah Jehan the conqueror and the friend of the Sesodia princes and himself the most splendid figure in his own brilliant court ? In either case what wonder, when the speaker looked to the East and South at the two dark thunder clouds of which one or other would assuredly hide for ever the sun of Islam, if his heart was filled with bitterness to the brim and if, in the words of the Hebrew prophet, he was mad for sight of his eyes which he saw !